The
HEARTH TAX,
other later Stuart Tax Lists
and the
ASSOCIATION OATH ROLLS

Compiled by

Jeremy Gibson
Senior Research Fellow, Roehampton Institute London

SECOND EDITION

With a Foreword by

Margaret Spufford
Research Professor of Social and Local History,
Roehampton Institute London

Federation of Family History Societies
in association with Roehampton Institute London

First published 1985 by the Federation of Family History Societies.

Second edition published 1996 by
Federation of Family History Societies (Publications) Ltd., c/o The Benson Room,
Birmingham and Midland Institute, Margaret Street, Birmingham B3 3BS, England
in association with Roehampton Institute London.

ISBN 1 86006 018 8

Computer typesetting, layout and cartography by Jeremy Gibson and Elizabeth Hampson.
Printed by Parchment (Oxford) Limited.

Acknowledgments

This Guide was first prepared more than a decade ago with the approval of the Keeper of Public Records, and I am grateful for the facilities provided, and for permission, with that of the Controller of Her Majesty's Stationery Office, for the use of anything that might be construed as Crown copyright. My thanks go also to the Scottish Record Society and Dr. Duncan Adamson for permission to use information on the Scottish Hearth Tax published in S.R.S. vol. 9, N.S., 1981; and to Cliff Webb and the Society of Genealogists for permission to use the list of Association Oath Roll class numbers first published in the *Genealogists Magazine*.

It would have been impossible to contemplate compiling the Guide without Mrs Jane Cox's generous offer of the use of her room at Chancery Lane, where I was able to examine dozens of documents on each of many visits to the Public Record Office. This meant considerable inconvenience to her and various colleagues who had to take turns at invigilation. I am enormously grateful to them all, and to those behind the scenes who had to produce so many records. I hope they will feel the end result has made it worthwhile.

Many others who helped me in different ways in the preparation of the first edition were acknowledged in that. For this new edition it has been unnecessary to call on so many, but once again archivists throughout the country have responded to my request for any additional information, especially on publications, transcripts and indexes. Whilst details of the actual records are unlikely to change (though a few more have come to light), the years since the first edition was prepared have seen *Hearth Tax* returns published for Essex (index only), Hampshire, Nottinghamshire, Rutland, the whole of Yorkshire, and Glamorgan; with transcripts (hopefully leading to publication) made for Cambridgeshire, Hertfordshire, Kent, Monmouthshire, and Northamptonshire; and *Association Oath Rolls* published for Derbyshire, Surrey and Jersey.

Tom Arkell has been particularly helpful with this new edition, providing, from his own examinations, corrections to dating of various returns, and drawing to my attention the need to identify the various towns which were sometimes (though not invariably) assessed separately from the counties in which they lay.

Preparation of this second edition, typeset rather than typewritten, meant retyping on to disc, carried out with meticulous accuracy by Beth Hampson. The maps which so enhance this edition were mostly first prepared for my recent Guide to *Protestation Returns*, but also include a map of Wales based on information kindly provided by John Rowlands.

Lastly, but most gratifyingly, I thank Margaret Spufford for her Foreword. This new edition is published in association with Roehampton Institute London, where, as Research Professor of Local and Social History, she has initiated the project she describes. It is my privilege to be involved with this, and to hope this new edition (which has already benefitted from Alastair Hawkyard's survey of microfilm of Hearth Tax records available from the P.R.O.) will further the study of these records.

J.S.W.G.

CONTENTS

FOREWORD

It is utterly unnecessary for me to introduce one of Jeremy Gibson's Guides, which are so often the first reference tool an historian (whether national, economic, social, local or family) consults for a quick overview before embarking upon a new project.

However, this new edition of *The Hearth Tax and Other Later Stuart Tax Lists* has a particular interest for me, because it is jointly published with Roehampton Institute London. We are very pleased that Mr Gibson has recently joined the History Department as a Senior Research Fellow. This is because we have a Departmental Project of great ambition. First, we want to produce a computerised base-map of the old ecclesiastical parishes for all the counties of England and Wales. This will be of use not only for mapping and analysis of the Hearth Tax but also for other taxation returns before boundary reform. Secondly, we want to analyse the population densities of those taxed, and, where possible, those exempt from taxation, and produce maps for the 1660s and 1670s for the whole country.

Between 1541 and 1650, the population of England and Wales almost doubled from two and three quarter millions to five and a quarter millions. This huge rise in population has made until now the wholesale analysis of the Hearth Taxes beyond the scope of the most enterprising research student. After the pioneering work of C.A.F. Meekings, Tom Arkell has done most to make the tax assessible to us. Christopher Husbands, who wrote in 1987 'Alone amongst mid and late seventeenth century taxes, the Hearth Tax allows historians to draw general, comparative conclusions about local economies', has undertaken an analysis of chargeable households for 859 randomly-sampled communities, which he has most generously now given to the Institute. However, as he wrote in 1992, 'Much of the potential of the Hearth Tax to provide a general framework for the socio-economic history of the later seventeenth century still remains to be exploited at both local and national levels.'

As a first step towards this huge ambition, we want to publish a series of county volumes in conjunction with the local Record Societies, where the Hearth Tax returns are not already adequately published. The Council of the British Record Society has expressed strong interest in such a scheme. Mrs Nesta Evans, the General Editor of the Index Library for the B.R.S., who has also recently become a Senior Research Fellow of Roehampton Institute, has already embarked on a transcript of the Michaelmas 1664 return for Cambridgeshire. Mr Gibson himself is working on the 1662 Oxfordshire return to compare with that for 1665.

We hope to publish a complete transcript of at least one return for each county, where one is not already in print. Ideally, finance permitting, we would like to be able to compare, as for Nottinghamshire, returns from the two main survival periods, 1662-1666 and 1669-1674. Returns published as part of this project will be accompanied by statistical tables of analysis of the remaining returns.

The results of these will, we hope, be mapped. Dr Susan Rose of Roehampton Institute has a pilot mapping project of the Hearth Tax in Surrey almost completed. We are fortunate in benefitting from the general advice and criticism of Tom Arkell, the acknowledged authority on the Taxes. We hope shortly to have Mrs Elizabeth Parkinson, who is already known for her edition of the Glamorgan Hearth Tax, working on a Ph.D. under his direction on the administration of the taxes. Alasdair Hawkyard is untying palaeographical knots for us; and we are collaborating with others working on hearth tax transcripts with view to publication.

We hope at Roehampton that this project will, in the end, make the results of this vast set of taxation returns available not only as an *index nominum* for at least one date for historians of kinship, surnames and family, and genealogists, but also for historians interested in relative taxable wealth and its distribution in England in the 1660s and the 1670s. But the whole huge edifice is built on the foundation of this Guide.

Margaret Spufford, O.B.E., Litt.D., F.B.A.
Research Professor of Social and Local History, Roehampton Institute London.

INTRODUCTION

This guide is primarily designed to tell family and local historians of the existence of records of the period 1660-1715, resulting from national legislation, which contains lists of **names**. They are mostly the names of tax-payers (and of those who did not pay the taxes, for various reasons), but the Association Oath Rolls, names of those who swore loyalty to the Crown in 1695, are also included.

It is **not** intended as a definitive guide to the taxation records of the period. Researching family and local history, one seeks the names of individuals. Knowledge of them is usually scanty. Their appearance in some of these lists will add to that knowledge: that they existed at all; that they were alive at that time; that they were living in such a place. Their discovery can lead to other more informative records. But their absence proves little or nothing. It is a lucky dip. With a basic research reason of this nature, there is no need for a prior study of the taxes concerned, on whom they were levied or why. Once names of interest are found, it may well be the researcher will want to find out more about the records in which they appear. In the Select Bibliography (page 12) and throughout this Guide there are references to works providing such information, but knowledge of the taxation methods is not a prerequisite of their use.

The Taxes

The majority of the taxes and their records relate to the reign of Charles II (1660-1685), of which the Hearth Tax generated by far the most (surviving) records, and consequently is the best known and most useful. Others were the 1661 Free and Voluntary Present to the King, Subsidies and Aids, and the Poll Tax. On the accession of William and Mary, the Hearth Tax was repealed (1689), being replaced eventually by the Land Tax and the Window Tax - few records of which survive pre-1715, and these only for the more prosperous - and, for a short time, the 'Marriage Tax', which is of great use and interest to genealogists, but unfortunately only exists for a few places.

Records of the first three are, generally, in the Public Record Office, and, for others, as occasional survivals in local record offices. These also sometimes have locally held copies of the Hearth Tax, and of course some have microfilm of nationally held records.

Of the records at the Public Record Office, the Association Oath Rolls are in Class C.213. The tax records are virtually all in Class E.179, Exchequer K.R. Lay Subsidy Rolls, dating from the reign of King John. From 1660 few were either Subsidies or confined to the laity, but for the purpose of the P.R.O. they are so categorised. The E.179 typescript calendar was published by the List and Index Society, vols. 44 (Beds. - Essex), 54 (Glos. - Lincs), 63 (London - Somerset), 75 (Staffs. - Yorks), 87 (Wales, Cinque Ports, Royal Household) (1969-1973), so is available in a few large libraries. The calendar indicates which tax records include lists of tax payers ('Names') and well over a thousand of these documents have been examined and are included in this Guide. Anyone studying E.179 records in any depth should refer to this calendar, as they may well find further references of use to them given there; and there are other Exchequer records relevant to these taxes which I have not attempted to locate or consult.

Against each document in the Public Record Office the reference or call number is shown in *square* brackets. When referring to or ordering up such records, the class number **E.179** (or **C.213** for Oath Rolls) **must** precede this. The figure in *round* brackets refers to the *very* approximate number of persons named. This has been calculated in an attempt to show the extent of any document and thus its likely use to the researcher. It cannot be emphasised too strongly that the figures are based on an extremely cursory examination, especially in the case of the longer records, and may easily be out by many hundreds or even thousands. Anyone requiring such totals must re-examine the documents to reach an accurate figure.

1. *The Free and Voluntary Present to King Charles II*. This was one of the first attempts by Parliament to raise money for the King on his restoration. Although it was voluntary, most of the better-off did subscribe. The money was collected, in the form of promises or cash, generally in towns on market days, in the autumn of 1661, with an occasional 'follow-up' record for slow payers the following year. In some cases occupations are given. Response was variable, often probably depending on the zeal of the collector. In Surrey just over half of those chargeable in due course under the Hearth Tax subscribed to the 'Present'. In contrast, at Banbury almost as many appear in each: 167 subscribers (ten of whom do not appear in the tax records) to 190 taxpayers. Returns survive for over thirty English and Welsh counties, and this neglected source would repay attention, if only for comparison with the Hearth Tax.

2. *The Hearth Tax*. This was imposed in 1662. Occupiers of houses (rather than owners) were taxed 2s. on each of their hearths, to be collected in two instalments, due at Lady day ('L') (25th March) and Michaelmas ('M') (29th September). The poor were exempt, but nevertheless were often listed. In later returns (1664-66) they were often shown separately, and in the early 1670s there were special printed forms on which parish officials could list those so exempt. The first collection was at Michaelmas 1662. That summer parish constables drew up the first lists of householders with the number of hearths each possessed. These paper lists sometimes survive in the E.179 records, and, if sorted and in good repair, are particularly useful. Although the handwriting may be semi-literate at times, the constables had first hand knowledge of those they were listing, so the names will be at their most accurate. The better-written rolls prepared for the Quarter Sessions, one copy for retention and the other to be forwarded to the Exchequer, are subject to transcription errors and ignorance of the names being copied.

The Hearth Tax continued until 1689, but because of the different authorities responsible at different times, records were returnable to the Exchequer only from Michaelmas 1662 to Lady Day 1666 and again from Michaelmas 1669 to Lady Day 1674. Occasional records outside these dates are found both in the P.R.O. and in local record offices.

In this Guide no discrimination is made between 'assessments' and 'returns'. The assessment was the list drawn up to show what people were expected to pay, the return was what they actually did pay - but the assessment was often marked with the payments, thus becoming the return. For the purpose of most users the names and number of hearths are shown in either. For assessments after 1662, and in particular in 1664, the 1662 list was copied for the use of the collectors, and thus a 1664 return will probably list the 1662 house-holders, annotated to show changes in occupation, increases or decreases of hearths, etc.

The 1662 list is often found to have names of more householders than those of later years, or at least a greater number of hearths assessable. At Banbury there were 190 in comparison with 146 and 138 at the two 1665 returns. However, those of the 1670s may show more, because of greater population, prosperity or efficiency on the behalf of the assessors. Much depends on whether lists of the exempt poor, sometimes as separate exemption certificates, are included.

There are often returns of 'arrears' for 1662-65. These are normally of use only to those studying the tax in depth. Whilst the tax assessments/returns will be in English (possibly with roman numerals for the hearths) and in secretary or other normal contemporary handwriting, these lists of arrears are more formal legal documents, in Latin and in the less familiar court hand. Usually relatively few names are given in any case ('constables' arrears' only list the constables themselves). There are exceptions, when a great number of the poor, who should have been exempt, had in fact been included in the original assessment; such cases will be evident from the figure given for those named.

Single returns for complete counties in England have now been published for Bedfordshire, Cornwall, Derbyshire, Devon, Dorset, Hampshire, Leicestershire, Norfolk, Nottinghamshire, Oxfordshire, Rutland, Shropshire, Somerset, Staffordshire, Suffolk, Surrey, Westmorland, and the whole of Yorkshire; and in Wales, Glamorgan, Merionethshire, and Pembrokeshire.

Transcription is completed or in progress (with hopes of publication in due course) for Cambridgeshire, Hertfordshire, Kent, and Northumberland. Editions comparing all surviving returns have been produced for the Isle of Wight, north east Warwickshire, the Ealing area of Middlesex and for Banbury in Oxfordshire; and an edition comparing the 1662 and 1665 returns for Oxfordshire is in preparation. The return for Worcester for 1678-80, outside the normal survival period for the tax records, is a significant recent volume for a specific place. There are indexes for Essex (published on microfiche), Kesteven in Lincolnshire, and Warwickshire.

Full bibliographical details of all these are given under the appropriate counties, with comments on their usually excellent and detailed introductions. They will give the interested researcher the information on the tax and its administration which is intentionally omitted here.

A major research project at the Roehampton Institute London, which will hopefully lead to more publications, is described in Professor Margaret Spufford's Foreword. Tables and maps showing, in simplified form, the survival, transcription and publication of returns are on pp. 8-11.

3. *Subsidies.* These had been the main means of raising money before the Civil War, and they occur again during the 1660s. Collection was by instalments, so they are difficult to date precisely. Only the wealthier members of the community were affected, gentry, landowners, the more substantial tradesmen. Distinction was made between taxation on goods ('moveables') and land. The amounts paid had become stereotyped and did not relate closely to real wealth, but are still an indication of status. In Banbury forty were assessed compared with four times that number in the Hearth Tax. Extant records are in the P.R.O., often in poor repair.

4. *Aids, or Monthly Assessments.* As the counties were responsible for raising fixed quotas, lists of the taxpayers were not forwarded to the Exchequer, and records at the P.R.O are rare. Surviving lists are in city and borough archives, particularly London, Bristol, Shrewsbury *etc*.

5. *Poll Tax.* A tax which can list not just the head of household but also his family and servants. Raised in 1660, 1667, 1678, 1689, 1691, 1694 and 1697. Very rarely survives, mainly in city archives, though the P.R.O. has occasional lists,and, more frequently, lists of defaulters - which, though only relating to very few people, give interesting evidence of mobility.

6. *'Marriage Tax', 1695-1706.* A tax levied on burials, births and marriages, bachelors over 25 and childless widowers. Effectively can give a census of the whole population, but, with the exception of some Wiltshire parishes, records only survive in borough archives. Those for Bristol has been published, and an index to London within the walls. Others have been found at Leicester, Oxford, Shrewsbury and Southampton.

7. *Land Tax.* A major tax, instituted about 1692-3 and continuing in some form until mid 20th century (see *Land and Window Tax Assessments*, in this series). Only occasional pre-1715 survivals, in local record offices. Only landowners likely to be listed.

8. *Window Tax.* From 1696. Very few lists, in local record offices, and probably few names in these (see *Land and Window Tax Assessments*).

9. *Other taxes.* Occasional lists for other taxes, may have been brought to my attention and so have been included here (i.e. Bedfordshire).

Often it is not clear for which tax the assessment is, so, apart from the Hearth Tax, the categories under which they are shown may be incorrect.

10. *Association Oath Rolls, 1695-6.* Class C.213 in the Public Record Office. These are described and listed by Cliff Webb in the *Genealogist's Magazine*, vol. 21, no. 4, December 1983, pp.120-123. This was an oath of loyalty to the Crown to be taken by all office-holders, but open for all to sign if they wished. In some places all males of some age and standing were encouraged to take the Oath and their names enrolled, together with those of defaulters. There are 473 rolls and they have not been individually examined.

HEARTH TAX RETURNS: ENGLAND AND WALES, 1662 - 1675.

Key:

'All' = County, not necessarily complete, and perhaps omitting some towns; when 'All' is used against a named town or area, then it relates only to those places.

Bold type = Published.

Italics = Microfilm or photocopy of original available.

Bold italics = Unpublished transcript available.

(2) following an entry = returns for both Lady Day and Michaelmas.

* following a date = in poor condition.

County	1662	1663	1664	1665	1666	1667	1669	1670	1671	1672	1673	1674/5
Bedfordshire	All*	Part	All	All(2)	Part	-		-	All(2)	-	-	-
Berkshire	All	*All*	All(2)	-	-	-	-	-	-	-	-	-
Bucks.	All?*	Part	-	-	-	-	-	-	-	Part	-	-
Cambs.	*All*		***All***		*All*	-	-	All*	Part*	-	-	***All***
Cheshire	All*	**Part**	*All*	Part	-	-	-	-	All	-	-	*All*
Note. Northwich Hd. 1664 published.												
Chester	-	*All*	*All*	**All**	-	-	-	-	-	-	-	-
Cornwall	All*	-	**All**	-	Part	-	-	-	-	-	-	-
Cumberland	All	-	***All***	-	-	-	-	-	-	-	All*(***Carlisle***)	-
Derbyshire	All*	-	**All**	-	-	-	-	**All**	-	Most	-	-
Devon	Part	-	Part*	-	-	-	-	-	-	-	Part	**All**
Exeter	All*	-	?	-	-	-	-	-	All	All	All	All
Dorset	-	All	**All**	-	-	-	-	-	-	-	-	All*
Co. Durham	All	*All*	*All*	*All*	*All*	-	-	All*	-	-	-	*All*
Essex	***All*** (index)	-	Part	Part(2)	Part(2)	Part	-	-	*All*	*All*	*All*	*All*
Glos.	Part	-	All	-	-	-	-	-	All*	All*	-	-
Bristol	All		All*	All	All	All	All	All	All	All	All	-
Hampshire	-	-	All	**All**	-	-	-	-	-	-	All*	All*
Isle of Wight	-	-	**All**	**All**	-	-	-	-	-	-	**All**	**All**
Southampton	**All**	-	-	-	-	-	-	**All**	-	-	-	-
Herefordshire	All	-	**All(2)**	**All(2)**	All	-	-	All*	-	-	All	-
Hertfordshire	*All*	*All(2)*	Part		Part	-	-	-	-	-	All*	-
Hunts.	-	-	All(2)	-	**All**	-	-	*All (to 1673)**	-	-	-	***All***
Kent	All(?)	Part(?)	**All**	-	-	-	-	-	-	All	-	Part(?)	-
Lancashire	Part*	*All*	*All*	-	*All*	-	-	-	-	-	*All(?)*	-
Leics.	Part*	-	**All(2)**	All(2)	**All**	-	-	*All*	-	-	-	-
Lincs.	Part	-	All(?)	**Part**	-	-	-	***Part***	Part	-	-	-
Lincoln	All	-	-	-	--	-	-	-	-	-	-	-
London	-	All	-	-	All	-	-	-	One pre-1674		-	All*
Middlesex	Part	All*	Part*	-	All	-	-	-	-	-	-	All
Westminster	probably as for Middlesex, but also 1675											
Monmouths.	-	All	All	-	-	-	-	-	-	-	-	-
Norfolk	-	-	**All**	-	**Part**	-	-	-	-	All*	-	-
Norwich	All*	-	-	-	**All**	-	-	-	-	-	-	-
Northants.	*All*	Part	-	-	-	-	-	*All*	-	-	-	*All*
Northumbd.	All*	-	***All***	All(2)	All	-	-	-	-	-	-	All
Note. 1664 in course of publication.												
Berwick	-	-	-	-	All	-	-	-	-	-	-	All
Newcastle	-	-	All(2)	**All**	All	-	-	All	-	-	-	All
Notts.	All	-	**All**	-	-	-	-	**Part**	-	-	-	**All**
Nottingham	All	-	-	-	-	-	-	-	-	-	-	**All**
Oxfordshire	***All***	-	-	All(2)	-	-	-	-	-	-	-	-
Note. 1662 for publication.												

County	1662	1663	1664	1665	1666	1667	1669	1670	1671	1672	1673	1674/5
Rutland	-	-	*All*	All(2)	-	-	-	-	-	-	-	-
Shropshire	All*	All(?)		-	-	-	-	-	-	All	-	-
Somerset	-	-	-	Part	-	-	-	-	-	-	-	-
Staffordshire	Part	-	-	All	-	-	-	-	-	All	All	-
Lichfield	-	-	All	-	-	-	-	-	-	-	All (?date)	
Suffolk	**Part**	All	All	-	-	-	-	-	-	-	-	**All**
Ipswich	Part	Part	-	All	(?)-	-	-	-	-	-	-	-
Surrey	All	Part	**All**	Part	Part	-	Part			All	All	-
Sussex	-	-	**Part**	**Part**	-	-	-	*All*	-	-	-	-
Warwickshire	All	All	*All*		*All*	-	-	*All*	Part	-	*All*	*All*

Note. Hemlingford, Tamworth and Atherstone Divisions published 1662-1674.

County	1662	1663	1664	1665	1666	1667	1669	1670	1671	1672	1673	1674/5
Westmorland	-	Part*	All	-	-	-	-	**All**	-	-	-	Part
Wiltshire	All*	-	-	-	-	-	-	-	-	-	-	-
Worcs.	*All*	-	*All*	*All*	*All*	-	-	-	*All*	*All*	-	*All*
Worcester	-	-	*All*	*All*	-	-	-	-	-	-	*All*	*All*

Note. Worcester City published for **1679-80**.

Yorkshire:

	1662	1663	1664	1665	1666	1667	1669	1670	1671	1672	1673	1674/5
York & Ainsty	-	-	-	All	-	-	-	City	City	**All**	-	All
East Riding	*Part*	-	*All**	-	-	-	-	*All*	-	**All**	*All(?)*	*All*
Hull	-	-	*All*	-	-	-	-	-	-	-	**All(2)**	-
North Riding	All	Part	Part	-	-	Part	-	All	Part	Part(?)	**All**	Part(?)
West Riding	Part	Part	All	-	Part	-	-	All	-	**All**	-	All

WALES

County	1662	1663	1664	1665	1666	1667	1669	1670	1671	1672	1673	1674/5
Anglesey	*All**	-	*All*	-	-	-	-	*All*	-	-	*All*	-
Breconshire	-	-	All*		Also one undated							
Caernarvons.	*All*	-	*Part*	-	-	-	-	All*	-	-	-	-
Cardiganshire	-	-	-	-	-	-	-	*All*	-	All	-	-
Carmarthens.	-	-	-	-	-	-	-	*All*		Another undated		
Denbighshire	-	-	All*	-	*All*	-	-	-		Part undated		
Flintshire	-	-	All*	-	-	-	-	*All*	-	-	-	-
Glamorgan	-	-	-	*All*	-	-	-	**All**	-	**Part**	**One undated**	
Merioneth	**All**	-	-	-	*All*	-	-	-	-	-	-	-
Montgomerys.	*All*	-	-	-	-	-	-	-	*All*	-	-	-
Pembrokes.	-	-	-	-	-	-	-	**All**	All*	-	-	-
Radnorshire	One 'All' undated.											

The Documents

In the absence of an alternative description, it should be assumed that a document will be a parchment roll, in good repair, and adequately legible - in secretary hand or ordinary later seventeenthth century handwriting. The rolls usually consists of membranes (ms.) around 2-2½ feet in length and 8 inches wide (obviously with many variations). They may hold up to 70-90 entries per column, sometimes more than one column and often written on both sides. They are either stitched just at the head, one on top of another, or head to foot, in one long and often unwieldy roll. Occasionally they have been flattened and then are easier to consult.

Sometimes the collectors were issued with a paper book (particularly the Hearth Tax in 1664) and these, if in good repair, are very much easier to work with.

Comments such as 'VG' relate to the condition and legibility of documents, not to the accuracy or coverage of their content.

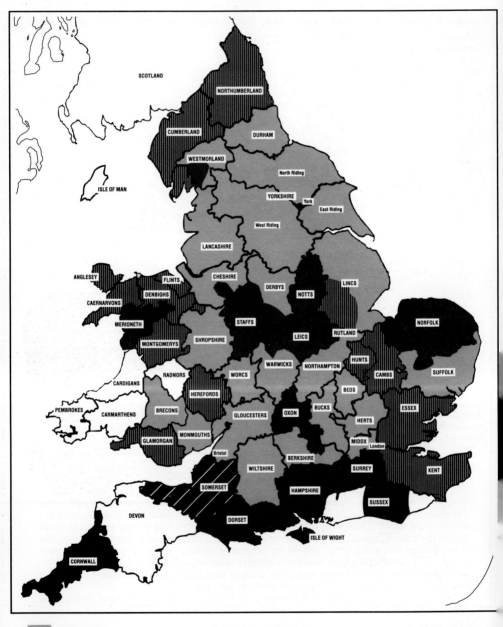

HT extant

Transcribed

Published

1662 - 1666

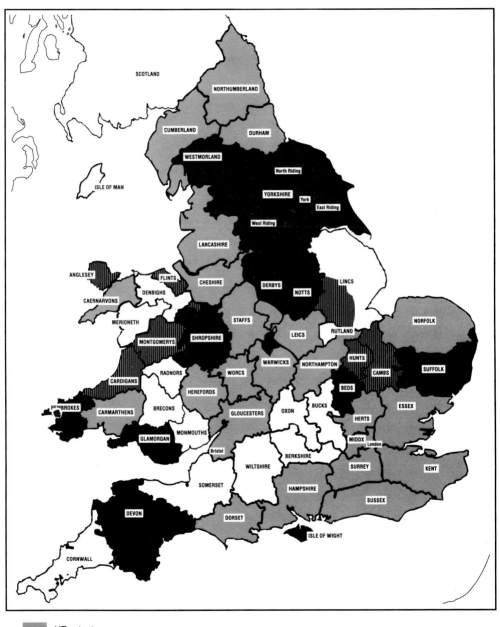

HT extant

Transcribed

Published

1669 - 1675

Although the *Association Oath* was taken in Scotland and probably in Ireland, rolls do not survive at the Public Record Office in Dublin nor at the Scottish Record Office (except for members of Parliament). Locally made lists of signatories in Scotland might be found dispersed among private muniments, court records or burgh records.

The Hearth Tax and Poll Tax in Scotland and the Hearth Tax in Ireland are described under the appropriate sections, pages 58 on.

The late C.A.F. Meekings, on the staff of the P.R.O., did a great deal of work on the Hearth Tax records, and frequently brief introductions and contents lists by him will be found attached to the documents. These are indicated by the initials 'CAFM'.

Dating. Where possible the documents have been given a precise calendar year date, and, with the Hearth Tax, 'L' or 'M' for the Lady Day and Michaelmas collections. These can be confused by returns covering more than one collection, and by bearing dates of the actual time the document and money was sent in, or the assessment was prepared. Sometimes the only date found is a regnal year (fortunately the regnal year for Charles II was from 30th January, so mostly coincides with the calendar year, N.S.), and it is these that are used in the P.R.O's list. In these cases the calendar year is shown in brackets.

It is impossible in compiling a Guide of this nature to give much attention to individual documents. Further information from those using them will be very welcome, even if only correction of the number of individuals named or more detail on coverage (and places missing). I will also be very glad to hear of other tax lists for the period, whether in national or local records, and of other transcripts and indexes, published or unpublished. With such a mass of figures and place-names, mistakes are bound to have occurred, and I will be most grateful for corrections to references or spellings.

J.S.W.G.

SELECT BIBLIOGRAPHY

Alldridge, Nick (ed), *The Hearth Tax: Problems and Possibilities*, Humberside College of Higher Education, for CORAL, 1983 (conference papers).

Beckett, J.V., *Local Taxation: National Legislation and the Problems of Enforcement*, Standing Conference for Local History, 1980.

Braddick, M.J., *Parliamentary Taxation in Seventeenth-Century England: Local Administration and Response*, Royal Historical Society Studies in History 70, The Boydell Press, 1994, pp. 231-270.

Chandaman, G.D., *The English Public Revenue 1660-1688*, Oxford, 1975.

Cressy, David, *Literacy and the Social Order: Reading and writing in Tudor and Stuart England*, C.U.P., 1980, pp. 96-103.

Fieldhouse, R., 'The Hearth Tax and other records', *Group Projects in Local History*, ed. A. Rogers. 1977.

Meekings, C.A.F. (introduction), *The Hearth Tax 1662-1689*, Exhibition of records (P.R.O., 1962).

Patten, John, 'The Hearth Taxes, 1662-1689', *Local Population Studies*, No.7, Autumn 1971, pp.14-27.

Schurer, Kevin and Arkell, Tom, *Surveying the People: The interpretation and use of document sources for the study of population in the later seventeenth century*, A Local Population Studies Supplement, Leopard's Head Press, 1992.

West, John, *Village Records*, 2nd edn., Phillimore, 1982, pp.131-33.

Most of the publications listed under county sections have good and detailed introductions. These and those listed above will have many further bibliographic references.

BEDFORDSHIRE

Publication

Hearth Tax **1670M** (wrongly described as 1671L) [P.R.O. E.179/72/301] (9,500) in Beds. Hist. Record Soc. **16**, 1934, as Appx. (pp. 65-159) to 'The Rural Population of Bedfordshire 1671-1921', Lydia M. Marshall; reprinted 1990. Includes exempt poor and empty houses. Indexed. Accompanying article mainly comparison of C17 and C19 population; no apparent comment on or comparison with other HT records.

Public Record Office [E.179]

***Free and Voluntary Present*, 1661-2**
County [243/6] (1,250), parchment roll; arrears [243/7] (100), paper sheets.

Hearth Tax (Assessments and returns)

1662M. County [72/297a] (5,000). Stodden and Willey hds. missing. Some ms. badly decayed; entries badly faded in parts; modern list of parishes and ms. nos.
1663L. Westoning [243/8] (1,000). Paper. Constables' returns, those exempt.
1664M. County [243/14] (5,000). Some decay repaired, variable legibility, some fading. Notes against entries relate to 1662M. Modern description and contents list.
1665L&M. County [72/298] (1,000). Variations. Valuable notes on reasons for not paying, i.e. in prison, no distress to be taken. Dated 12 April 1666.
(1666). Stodden, Clifton,Barford, Wixhamtree hds. [243/9] (5,000). Paper, repaired, bound. Annotated.
Flitt, Manshead, Biggleswade, Redbornstoke hds. [243/10] (2,500). Paper book, repaired, annotated. VG.
1670M . County [72/301] (9,500). *Published.*
1671(L?). County [72/302] (9,500). Badly decayed; otherwise legibility adequate.
(Arrears)
1664L. County [370/1] (30). Latin.
1663-4. Miscellaneous. [358].

Subsidies
(1660). Wixhamtree, Clifton, Biggleswade hds. [72/296] (400).
1661. Manshead hd. [72/297] (900). Parts badly faded, variable legibility.
(1673). Barford, Stodden, Willey hds. [72/306] (500). Poor legibility.

Association Oath Rolls, **1695-6** [C.213]
[2] County; [3] Bedford.

Bedfordshire Record Office, Bedford

Hearth Tax
1665. Part of **Manshead hd.**: Billington, Houghton Regis, Toddington, Tilsworth, Harlington, Totternhoe, Milton Bryan, Woburn [AD 3350 pp. 15-18].
c.1683. Northill, incl. the hamlets of Ickwell, Over or Upper Caldecote, Nether or Lower Caldecote, Thorncote, Hatch, Brook End, Beeston [HY 823].

Poll Tax
1689-90. Renhold [PO 14 p.19-20]. Copy CAMPOP.
1694. Aspley Guise [HW 41].

Aids:
1693. Cranfield [LL 7/3]; Maulden [LL 7/4].

Ship Money:
1677. Renhold [PO 14 p.8]; Cople [ABP/W 1684/20].

Weekes' Tax:
1707, 1715. Renhold [PO 14 p.40].

Certainty Money:
1712. Houghton Conquest [RA/324].

Land Tax: **1697,1706.** Renhold [PO 14 p.39].

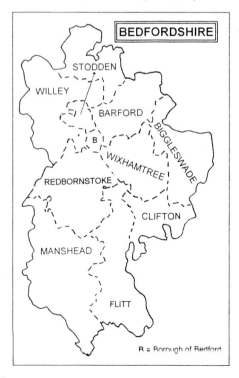

B = Borough of Bedford

BERKSHIRE

Publications

Hearth Tax, for **Reading St. Mary** and **St. Giles, 1664M** [P.R.O. E.179/76/460, formerly 76/458], **St. Laurence and Whitley 1663M** [243/25], **Caversham** (formerly Oxon.) **1662M** [255/4 (Oxon)] (total 510 names), in *The Hearth Tax for Reading and Caversham 1662-3*, transcibed and edited by Edgar Powell, 1913.

Hearth Tax, **Uffington, Baulking, Woolstone, Kingston Lisle, Fawler, 1663M** [P.R.O. E.179/243/25] in *Berkshire Tracts 1*, transcribed by J.E. Little.

Hearth Tax, **Wantage 1663M** [P.R.O. E.179/243/25] (144) in *Berkshire FHS Jnl*. **7.** 4 (Summer 1982).

Public Record Office [E.179].

Free and Voluntary Present, 1661-2
County [243/21] (2,500-3,000). Varying size rolls.

Hearth Tax *(Assessments and returns)*
(those available on microfilm from P.R.O. marked §)

1662M. County [243/24 §] (9,000). Constables' returns, paper, bound, VG.
 Moreton hd. (North and South divisions) and **Newbury** (town) [243/27] (2,000-3,000). Constables' assessments. Paper.
 Ganfield hd. [367/1] (25). Shillingford only.

Public Record Office: Hearth Tax continued

1663M. County [243/25 §] (9,000). Constables' returns, paper, loose. *Some published.*
 Ock Hd. [75/381] (365). Constables' returns, paper. Including exempt poor. Kilns listed for Sutton Courtenay. Dated 6 June 1664.
 Kintbury Eagle hd. [75/400] (250). Constables' returns, paper. Include exempt poor for Kintbury. Almsbury(?). Dated 5 March 1663 and 1 Nov 1664.

1664L. County [243/26 §] (5,000). Constables' returns, paper, bound in 3 books. VG.

1664M. County [76/460] (6,500). Patchy. Parts adequately legible, part badly faded or decayed: partially repaired. Modern contents list of hundreds. *Reading St. Mary, St. Giles, published.*

1663-64. County [358]. Very many loose paper returns by constables, unsorted.

Subsidies
No date. Beynhurst hd. [75/379] (150). Poor condition and legibility, faded in parts.
 Faircross hd. [76/459] (500). Badly faded in part.
 Kintbury Eagle hd. [243/28] (120). Bad condition poor legiblity. Possibly *Poll Tax*, not *Subsidy*.

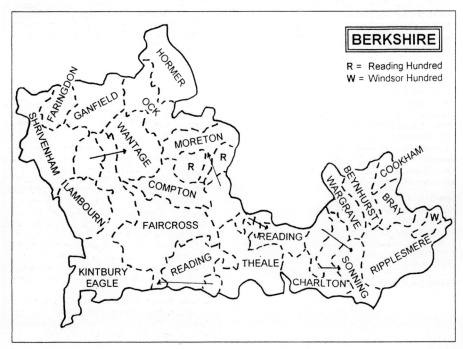

Berkshire: *Public Record Office* continued

Poll Tax
(1661). Cookham hd. [243/22] (100).
(1667). Newbury, Bagnor, Welford, Speenhamland. Certificates of defaulters [76/449b] (19).
1678 May. Aldermaston [76/454] (130). Bad handwriting.
June. Faringdon, Shrivenham, Ganfield, Wantage, Lambourn [76/456] (106). Collectors' names only.
June. Kintbury Eagle and Compton [76/455] (104). Collectors' names only.
July. Reading and Theale hds. [76/457] (57). Collectors' names only.

Association Oath Rolls, 1695-6 [c.213]

[4] County; [5] Vale of Berkshire; [6] Wantage; [7] New Windsor; [8] Reading; [9] Wallingford; [10] Abingdon; [11] Newbury; [12] Maidenhead; [13] Wokingham; [14] Easthampstead.

Berkshire Record Office, Reading

Hearth Tax
1663M. Photocopies of P.R.O. E. 179/243/25 [T/A 17/] for:
1 Newbury; 2 Abingdon; 3 Maidenhead; 4 Clewer; 5 New Windsor; 6 Whistley-in-Hurst; 7 Compton, East and West; 8 East Ilsley; 9 Yattendon; 10 Speenhamland; 11 Brightwalton; 12 Hinton Waldrist; 13 Cumnor, Wootton, Witham, North and South Hinksey (including Botley); 14 Hd of Hormer: Abingdon (Sandford, Northcourt, Shippon), Sunningwell, Kennington, Radley (incl. Thrupp), Besselsleigh, Grandpont; 15 Hd of Kintbury Eagle (north side) incl. Letcombe Regis and Bassett; 16 Sonning town; 17 Wallingford; 18 Winterbourne and Chieveley; 19 Maidenhead; 20 Wantage, Grove, Charlton; 21 Frilford, Lyford, East Hanney, Draycott Moor, Goosey, Fyfield, Garford, Appleton (incl. Eaton), Marcham, Kingston Bagpuize, Tubney; 22 Wokingham; 23 Hungerford; 24 Stanford-in-the-Vale; 25 Enborne.
Goosey. Photocopies of 1662M, P.R.O. E. 179/243/24 [T/A 35.3] and 1664M E. 179/76/460 [T/A 35.4].

Land Tax etc.
1679- . Brightwalton.
1704. Watchford, Woolhampton.

Society of Genealogists

Snell Collection, vol. 17 (MS) has indexed transcripts of Hearth Tax 1663-4 [P.R.O. E.179/243/25] for about 90 parishes.

BUCKINGHAMSHIRE

Publications

Langley Marish *Hearth Tax* 1663M (135), *Heritage* (Windsor/Slough FHS) 4, 3 (1981).
Great Hampden, *Poll Tax* 1660, *Subsidy/Aid*, 1668, 1673 [Bucks R.O. D/LE/17], *Origins* (Bucks FHS) 9, 2 & 3 (1985).
Burnham Hd. 'The account of subscriptions to the present to Charles II [1661-2] from the Hundred of Burnham', *Records of Bucks.*, 7, 1897
Stone. 'The *Association Oath Rolls* for Bucks., 1696', Wallace Gandy, *Records of Bucks.*, 11, 1920-26, pp. 109-20. Incl. transcript of Stone etc.

Public Record Office [E.179]

Free and Voluntary Present, 1661-2
County [80/333] (3,000). Paper book. *Burnham published.*

Hearth Tax (Assessments and returns)
1662M. Ashendon hd. [80/354] (900). Much decayed at foot and consequently patchy legibility.
Aylesbury (3 hds.) [80/348] (500). Many entries lost from decay, poor legibility, bad condition, repaired.
Buckingham (3 hds.) [244/16] (1,000). Decayed but repaired. Part badly faded or decayed, part fair legible.
Burnham hd. [80/350] (1,000). Repaired after bad decay. Hearths mainly lost; some names legible.
Cottesloe hd. [80/352] (1,000). Repaired but mostly illegible.
Desborough hd. [80/345] (70). Bad condition and legibility, unfit for production.
Newport (3 hds.) [80/349] (3,000). Decayed but repaired. Part good legibility, part faded or lost.
Stoke hd. [80/347] (900). Decayed but repaired. Some bad fading. Modern list of contents.
1662M-1664L County [224/11] (375). Constables' returns; paper.
County [80/351]. Variations schedule. Repaired but very poor and illegible.
1663-4. Stray constables' paper returns: (north) Edgcott, Twyford (2), Shalstone, Water Stratford. Tingewick, Preston Cowley, Thorndon, Turweston. Barton Hartshorn, Steeple Claydon, Hillesden, Westbury, Marsh Gibbon, (south) Aston Clinton, Buckland, Borton cum Broughton, Farnham Royal (2), Waterside in Chesham, Chalfont St. Peter, Taplow, Dorney, Bouny/Boueney, Burnham [358]
1672. Aylesbury hd. Haddenham, Little Kimble [224/12] (320). Constables' return, paper book.
?1672. Aylesbury hd. [244/15] (600). Paper book. similar to 244/12.
No date. Buckingham hd. (part) [367/1] (?100). Fragment. Bad condition.
(Arrears)
1674L. County [244/13] (300). Latin.

Buckinghamshire: *Public Record Office* contd

Subsidies
1663 Sep. Burnham hd. [80/335] (200). Repaired but most names partially lost through decay.
Nov. Desborough hd. [244/10] (65). Certificates of residence.
(1664). Aylesbury (3 hds.) [80/336] (500). Repaired. Some entries lost from decay; faded in parts, poor legibility.
Chiltern (3 hds.) [80/338] (1,000). 1m. badly faded (Durney and Burnham), but otherwise good legibility and condition
Cottesloe (3 hds.) [80/337] (200). Faded and decayed, repaired. Some parts legible.
Newport (3 hds.) [80/334] (1,500). Faded in parts, poor legiblilty.

Association Oath Rolls, 1695-6 [C.213]
[15-16] **County;** [17] Deputy Lieutenants and Militia Officers; [18] **Buckingham;** [19] **Chipping (High) Wycombe;** [20] **Aylesbury** (Stone etc *published*); [21] **Amersham;** [22] **Gt Marlow;** [23] **Wendover.** *Part published.*

Buckinghamshire Record Office, Aylesbury

Subsidies or Aids
Aylesbury hds., 1665 [D138/22/3]; 1668 [D/LE/17/8]; 1673 [D/LE/17/9]. *Great Hampden 1668 and 1673 published.*

Poll Tax
Aylesbury hds. 1660 [D/LE/17/3]. *Great Hampden published.*
Stoke hds., 1694, 1698-9 [D/W/89-90].
Cheddington, 1694 [D12/78].
Fulmer, 1698 [PR 81/28/1].

Land Tax etc.
West Wycombe: 1689, 1700, 1703, 1705, 1707, 1709, 1712, [PR 227/28/1].

Marriage Tax
Liberty of **Shipton Lee** in Quainton, 1696, [PR.169/28/6]. Copy CAMPOP
Quainton, 1702 [PR.169/28/6]. Copy CAMPOP.
Great Brickhill, various [PR.25/1/2].

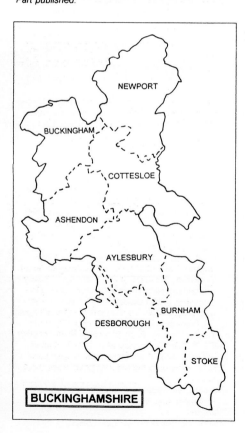

BUCKINGHAMSHIRE

CAMBRIDGESHIRE and ISLE OF ELY

Publications

Descriptive articles on the *Hearth Tax*, in the relevant volumes of the *V.C.H.*, by CAFM, with details of the P.R.O. documents in vol. **4**, p. 272. Analyses of totals but no names.

'Family History from Records of Property: *Hearth Tax*' Janet Hurst, *Jnl. Cambs FHS*, **2**, 5, Feb 1980).

Cambridgeshire Subsidy Rolls, 1250-1695 by W.M. Palmer (Norwich, 1912, reprinted from *The East Anglian*, 1898-1909) incl. lists for **Shingay-cum-Wendy, 1660, 1661**, pages 28-9, and for **Melbourn, 1672**, p.31.

Hearth Tax, **1674, Melbourn** and **Meldreth**, [presumably P.R.O. E.179/326/10] (216), in 'Some C17 Inhabitants of South West Cambs.', Janet Hurst, *Jnl. Cambs FHS*, **3**, 2 (May 1981), reprinted from articles in the *Congregational Magazine*, Jan 1895, reprinted in *A Nonconformist Bicentenary Memorial* (Cambridge Central Library).

Public Record Office [E.179]

(those available on microfilm from P.R.O. marked §; asterisked items are also on microfilm at the *Cambridgeshire C.R.O., Cambridge*)

Free and Voluntary Present, 1661-2
County [84/433]* (3,000). In 13 separate rolls (each separate ms. inside), by hundreds, etc.

Cambridgeshire: _Public Record Office_ continued

Hearth Tax (Assessments and returns)

1662M. County [84/436 §]* (9,000). Enrolled assessment listing all bound to pay (some subsequently exempt). Fewer names than later rolls. **Whittlesey** [244/24] (400). Paper book, repaired.

1664M/1665. County [84/437 §]* (17,000). Enrolled, thorough revision of 1662M. Almost as comprehensive as 1674L. Many comments, removals, new entries, those exempt. VG, but imperfect. Transcript in progress.

1666L. County [244/22 §]* (17,200). Returns, paper books made after the tax had been collected. Headings of 'Paid' and 'Unpaid'.

1670M. County [375/27, formerly 244/25] (5,000). Introduction by CAFM. Includes Cambridge town, Ely, Witchford, Wisbech, Armingford, Chesterton hds. Much decay, repaired, and fading, but legible and good in parts. Cambridge mainly illegible. Ely much decayed. Other hds. variable.

1671M-1673L. County [244/26] (300). Fragment of roll, bad condition and legibility.

1674L. County [244/23 §]* (13,500). Lists made by sub-collectors. Divided into taxpayers and those exempt by certificate. Fair copy; ms. bound at top, easy to use. Indexed transcript at _SofG_ and _CRO._

(Exemption certificates)

1671M. Armingford hd. [326/2] (740). Printed certificates, repaired, bound. Modern contents list.

1672/1673L. Chesterton, Northstow, Papworth hds. [84/440 §]* (3,500). Repaired and bound, modern contents list.

1674L. County [326/10] (200). Printed certificates, much decayed but repaired, bound. Modern contents list

Subsidies

(1663). County [244/21] (500). Fragment, bad condition parts legible but most illegible.

(1664). Chesterton, Northstow, Papworth hds. [84/435] (300).

Poll Tax

(1660). Armingford, Longstow, Thriplow, Wetherley hds. [83/429] (500). Poor condition and legibility.

Flendish, Staine, Staploe, Thriplow, Wetherley hds. [83/430] (70). Names of constables only.

Flendish hd. [83/431] (100).

Isle of Ely [83/432] (100). Names of collectors and constables only.

Staine, Whittlesford hds. [244/20] (250). One membrane damaged by damp.

1678. Chilford hd. [84/444,446]* (85). Part faded; incomplete.

Longstow hd. [84/445]* (250). Decayed and faded, poor condition and legibility.

Association Oath Rolls, 1695-6 [C.213]
[24] Cambridgeshire; [25] Cambridge; [26] Isle of Ely.

Cambridgeshire Record Office, _Cambridge_

Microfilm of asterisked P.R.O. holdings.

Hearth Tax
Original: **1662M.** Guilden Morden.
Transcript: **Cambridge** borough, **1664, 1674.**
Subsidies
Littleport, 1662-3(4), 1663(2), 1671.
Poll Tax
Comberton, 1692.
Assessments for Aids and Taxes
Bassingbourn, 1692, 1698, 1711, 1712.
Trophy Tax for the drums and colours
Bassingbourn, 1690, 1694, 1706, 1715.
Land Tax
Bassingbourn, 1715; Comberton, 1707; Linton, 1694; Meldreth, 1699-1720.

Society of Genealogists

Hearth Tax:
1662M. Whittlesey.
1674L. County. Indexed transcript.

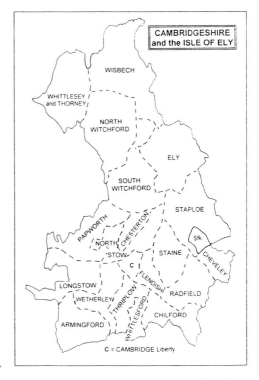

CAMBRIDGESHIRE
and the ISLE OF ELY

WISBECH

WHITTLESEY
and THORNEY

NORTH
WITCHFORD

ELY

SOUTH
WITCHFORD

STAPLOE

PAPWORTH

NORTH
CHESTERTON

STOW

STAINE

Sfk

CHEVELEY

C

LONGSTOW

FLENDISH

WETHERLEY

THRIPLOW

RADFIELD

CHILFORD

ARMINGFORD

WHITTLESFORD

C = CAMBRIDGE Liberty

CHESHIRE

Note. Chester was assessed separately from the County.

Publications

Northwich Hundred. Poll Tax 1660 and Hearth Tax 1664, Lancs and Ches. R.S., **119** (1979), ed. G.O. Lawton. Indexed. *Poll Tax* [P.R.O. E.179/244/30] (5,756); *Hearth Tax* [E.179/86/145] (2,585), separated into chargeable and exempt.

Hearth Tax, Chester, 1665M [P.R.O. E.179/86/146] (1,650), in 'Hearth Tax returns for the City of Chester, 1664-5', ed. F.C. Beazley, Lancs. and Ches. R.S. **52** (*Miscellanies*, vol. 5), 1906. Indexed. Arranged by ward. Includes changes and additions since 1662, also exempt poor. Short introduction.

Hearth Tax returns for **Eddisbury** and **Wirral** hds. are in volumes of *Cheshire Sheaf*, series 3. This was a monthly, bound and indexed in annual volumes. The indexes include names in the HT (take care not to consult the adjacent but separate indexes to apprenticeship indentures). HT lists are scattered through the issues, in numbered sections, also listed in annual contents list:

Wirral hd., 1663L [P.R.O. E.179/244/35 (compared against E.179/86/145)] in volumes 8 (1910) and 9 (1912), sections 1535-2097.

Eddisbury hd. Western div., 1663L [E.179/244/34] in volume 7 (1909), sections 1222-1347.

Eddisbury hd., Eastern and Western divs., 1664L [E.179/86/145], in volumes 11-13 (1914-16), sections 2452-2650, 2806-3243.

Part of **Broxton hd., 1663L** [E.179/244/34] is in volume 14 (1917), not apparently completed; this transcript excludes single hearth households.

Lymm, High Legh, Thelwall, 1673L&M, 1674L (230), in 'Hearth Tax Assessments of Lymm', M.N. Jackson, *North Cheshire FH*, **5**,2 (May 1978), pp. 46-49.

Public Record Office [E.179]

Free and Voluntary Present, 1661-2
Broxton hd. [244/32a] (1,250).
Bucklow hd. [86/159] (1,000).
Eddisbury hd. [244/32] (1,500).
Nantwich hd. [244/31] (1,200). Decayed and faded in parts.

Hearth Tax *(Assessments and returns)*
(those available on microfilm from P.R.O. marked §; * = microfilm at Cheshire R.O.)

1662M. County [86/141] (?5,000). Bad condition and legibility.
1663L. High constables' books, paper, for **Broxton** (1,750), **Eddisbury** (1,250), **Macclesfield** (3,000) hds [244/34]*; **Wirral hd.** (1,150) [244/35]*. Part *published.*
1663L-1664L. **Chester** [86/143]* (1,250). By ward. Includes decreases and exempt.

Public Record Office continued

1664L. County [86/145 §]* (24,000). VG, fair copy parchment book in sections. Chargeable and exempt separated. Eddisbury, Northwich hds. *published.*
Chester [86/1420* (1,250). By ward, exempt listed.
1665M Broxton [86/149]* (2,250), **Nantwich** [86/148]* (2,400), **Northwich** [86/150]* (3,000), **Eddisbury** and **Wirral** hds. [244/37]* (5,000). Fair copy parchment books. Includes changes in occupation, those exempt.
Chester [86/146]. *Published.*
County [358] (1,200). Paper. Defaulters, tabulated to show reasons. VG. Variations.
1671M. County [86/153] (1,250). Parchment book, annotated. Good.
1674L. County [86/155]* (10,000). VG. Parchment books.
(Exemption certificates)
1670, 1672, County [86/152] (4,000 for each year). VG, repaired and bound, mainly printed forms, in two books.
1674. County [326/5] (3,000). Printed paper forms. bound.
Chester [326/4] (371). Printed paper forms, bound.
(Arrears)
1663M. County [370/8] (100). Latin
1663. Chester [370/9,10] (50 and 50). Latin.
1664L. County [86/144]*(75). Latin.

Subsidies (* = microfilm at *Cheshire R.O.*)
1663. Wirral hd. [244/33]* (200). Parchment sheets, bad condition and legibility.
1660-69. Broxton hd. [86/151] (1,000). Fragments. some very bad, some legible.

Poll Tax
1660. Bucklow hd. [272/40] (400). Very bad condition, unfit for production
Chester [244/29] (2,400). Paper book.
Northwich [244/30] (5,756). *Published.*

Association Oath Rolls, 1695-6 [C.213]
[27-28] County; [29-31] **Chester** city;
[32] **Congleton.**

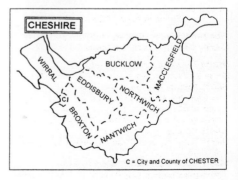

C = City and County of CHESTER

Cheshire continued

Cheshire continued

Cheshire Record Office, Chester

Microfilm of P.R.O. Hearth Tax holdings as asterisked, 1663-5, 1673-4.

Chester City Record Office, Chester

Hearth Tax
1672. Chester (whole city) [CAS/1].

Subsidies/Aids [CAS/1]
1662. Four wards +(?) St. Oswald's ward.
1664-5. Two wards only.
1664-5, 1666. Chester city.
1665. St. Michael's ward.
1673 , 1677, 1679, 1685, 1692, 1699, ?whole city, or at least some wards.

Poll Tax
1692, 1694, 1698. City (incomplete) [CAS/1].

Marriage Tax
1705. Chester (whole city) [CAS/2].

Land Tax
1704. Chester [CAS/2].

Manchester Central Library, Local Studies Unit

Subsidy: **1663.** Tintwistle, Transcript [LI/45/11/1].

CORNWALL

Publications

Cornwall Hearth and Poll Taxes, 1660-1664: Direct Taxation in Cornwall in the Reign of Charles II, ed. and pub. by T.L. Stoate, 1981. Full transcripts of *Hearth Tax* **1664M** [P.R.O. E.179/244/44] (14,500), *Free and Voluntary Present* **1661** [E.179/244/41], and *Poll Tax* **1660, Kerrier hd., East hd** (northern div.) [E.179/244/39], **Powder hd.** (eastern div.) [E.179/ 244/40]. All indexed. Detailed introduction and description of all P.R.O. E.179 records.

Public Record Office [E.179]

Free and Voluntary Present, 1661-2
County [244/41] (1,000). *Published.*

Hearth Tax (Assessments and returns)
(those available on microfilm from P.R.O. marked §)
1662M. County [89/356] (9,000). Decayed and repaired, ms. stitched at top. Bad condn. and leg. Intro. and contents list. Trigg and Penwith hds. missing. Virtually duplicated in [244/44], 1664M.
1664M. County [244/44 §]. *Published.*
1666L. Truro, St. Just, Creed [244/46] (200). Paper, repaired and bound.
1666M. Pyder hd. [244/42] (400). Paper, constables' returns, bound.

Cornwall: **Public Record Office** continued

Cornwall: **Public Record Office** continued

Hearth Tax (Arrears)
1662M [370/12,13] (80 and 50). Latin, mainly names of constables.
1664-66 (for 1662M) [370/14] (150). Latin.
(for 1664L) [370/15] (160). Latin
Subsidies
1663. Penwith hd. [89/348] (350).
Pyder hd. [89/346 and 244/43] (350).
West hd. [89/347] (750).

Poll Tax
1660. Kerrier and **East** (northern divn.) **hds.** [244/39] (8,000). Paper, bound, complete. *Published.*
Powder hd. (eastern divn.) [244/40] (5,500). Paper, bound. *Published.*
Pyder hd. [89/345] (1,000). Bad legibility.
(?1692). St. Agnes, part of St. Breock in Pyder [276/73a] (150). Variable.

Assessment or General Aid
1689. Pyder hd. [244/47] (1,000). Paper. Incl. Columb Major, Padstow, Newlyn, St. Agnes, St. Ervan, St. Breock, St. Enoder.
Pyder hd. [369/23] (110). Paper, repaired. Perranzabuloe, Little Colan.

Association Oath Rolls, 1695-6 [C.213]
[33-35] **County**, Grand Jury, tinners;
[36-37] **Launceston;** [38] **Liskeard;**
[39] **Lostwithiel;** [40] **Truro;** [41] **Bodmin;**
[42] **Helston;** [43] **Saltash;** [44] **Camelford;**
[45] **West Looe;** [46] **Grampound;** [47] **East Looe;**
[48] **Penryn;** [49] **Tregony;** [50] **Bossiney;**
[51] **St. Ives;** [52] **Fowey;** [53] **St. German;**
[54] **St. Michael;** [55] **St. Mawes;** [56] **Callington;**
[57] **Falmouth;** [58] **Penzance;** [59] **Marazion;**
[464] **Scilly Isles.**

CUMBERLAND

Public Record Office [E.179]

Free and Voluntary Present, 1661-2
County [90/73] (1,000).

Hearth Tax *(Assessments and returns).*

1662M. County [90/77] (7,500). Some ms. torn and
Carlisle at end, several ms. wanting. See also
245/3.
1662. County [245/3] (5,000). Small parchment ms.,
half badly decayed.
(1673). County [90/74] (10,000). Much decayed, but
repaired and flattened. Parts easily legible, other
parts faded and/or decayed.
1673M/1674L. County [90/76] (12,500).
Legibility generally good, but some poor. Includes
exempt poor.
(?year). [90/78] (350). Fragments, incl. Braithwaite,
Eskdale, Wastdale, Harrington, Briashat,
Workington, Stainbarne,. Varying condition and
legibility.
(Exemption certificates)
1673. County [326/6] (3,000). Printed paper forms,
bound.

Subsidies
(1663). County [245/1] (210). Poor condition.
1663 Feb. **Carlisle** [245/2] (16). Paper.
1664 Apr. **Allerdale ward** [90/75] (33).

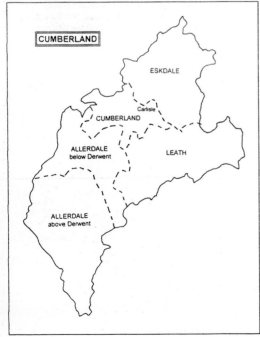

Public Record Office continued

Association Oath Rolls, 1695-6 [C.213]
[60-61] **County,** nonconformist ministers;
[62] **County,** Lord Lieutenant, etc.; [63] **Carlisle;**
[64] **Cockermouth;** [65] **Whitehaven.**

Cumbria Record Office, *Carlisle*

Hearth Tax
*c.***1664. County** (photostat copy and transcript).
1673. Carlisle (modern transcript).

DERBYSHIRE

Publications

Free and Voluntary Present, **County,
1661-2** [P.R.O. E.179/245/6], ed. David
Clay, Derbys FHS, 1992.
Hearth Tax, **County, 1662-70** [exact
coverage and original records shown
below], in *Derbyshire Hearth Tax Assess-
ments, 1662-70,* ed. David G. Edwards with
an introduction incorporating material by the
late C.A.F. Meekings, Derbyshire Record
Society, vol. **7**, 1982:
Appletree hd. (Spondon and Borrowash
only), **1662M** [P.R.O. E.179/93/378];
Appletree hd. (remainder of hd.) **1664L**
[P.R.O. E.179/94/405]. Incl. exempt poor.
Repton and Gresley hd., 1662M (most of
hd.) [P.R.O. E.179/245/7]; Winshill,
Repton, Rosliston, Coton only) [P.R.O.
E.179/94/378].
Repton and Gresley hd., 1664L (Walton
upon Trent only) [P.R.O. E.179/245/10].
Includes exempt poor.
**High Peak, Morleston and Litchurch,
Scarsdale,** and **Wirksworth hds., 1670**
[Derby Central Library, Derbyshire
Collection, DC 9953-56].
Fully indexed.
The admirable introduction gives a very
readable explanation of the mechanics of
the collection of the tax, and the
complexities of dating the returns. Table 1
shows the principal surviving Hearth Tax
records for the county., in the P.R.O. and in
Derby Central Library, with an indication of
completeness and/or legibility, date and
hundred. Pp. xviii-xxxv describe these in
detail, document by document, and forms
the basis for the brief notes below.

Derbyshire, Publications continued

Marriage Tax, **Melbourne, 1695** (660), Jnl. Derbys. Arch. & Nat. Hist. Soc., **7** (1885), pp. 1-30, with an introduction by R.E. Chester Waters. Indexed.

Public Record Office [E.179]

Free and Voluntary Present, 1661-2
County [245/6] (4,000). Published.

Hearth Tax (Assessments and returns)
(those available on microfilm from P.R.O. marked §)

1662M. County [94/378] (10,000). Exchequer duplicate. Appletree, Scarsdale hds. defective; Derby largely missing. Decayed, repaired, condition and legibility generally poor. Spondon and Borrowash; Winshill, Repton, Rosliston and Coton published.
Appletree hd. [245/8] (2,000). Exchequer duplicate, paper book, copy of 94/378 (only hd. surviving), but made for 1664M.
1662M/1664L. County [245/7] (10,000). Constables' paper returns, as 1662M, but made or confirmed in Oct 1664. Includes three arrears schedules. Bound as book. Introduction by CAFM. Easy to use (lengthy description in D.R.S. **7** pp.xix-xxiii). Repton and Gresley hd. published. M'film in Derby Library.
1664L. County. Exchequer duplicate. Exempt poor shown. Split into hds. with separate references:
Derby, Morleston and Litchurch hd. [94/401] (2,000). Outer ms. faded otherwise perfect. Markeaton missing.
Appletree hd. [94/405 §] (1,800). Dorse of m.11 and tails of mm.3 and 4 rubbed, otherwise perfect. Borrowash and Spondon missing, Shottle and Postern illegible. Published. Microfilm at Derby Central Library.
Scarsdale hd. [94/400] (3,600). Mostly perfect. Possibly 1m. missing.
Wirksworth hd. [94/402] (2,610). Perfect. Bonsall and Newton Grange missing.
High Peak hd. [94/403] (3,500). Some 80 entries illegible (mm.13,14,16,17), otherwise perfect.
Repton and Gresley hd. [245/10] (1,200). Decay, repaired, four ms. illegible in parts. Some ms. lost. Defective. Walton on Trent published.
For **1670**, see Derbyshire Central Library.
1672. Scarsdale hd. [94/394] (3,500). Exchequer duplicate. Place arranged alphabetically, preceded by Chesterfield; missing: Barlow, Beauchief, Calow, Tibshelf and Oxcroft, Walton, Wingerworth.
Appletree hd. [245/9/1] (1,800). Places arranged alphabetically. 2ms. missing, others partly illegible.
High Peak hd. [245/9/2] (2,650). Constablewicks in alphabetical order, places within them in no particular order. 3ms. missing, others partly illegible.
Wirksworth hd. [245/9/3] (1,600). Places arranged in alphabetical order, Ashbourne to Wensley and Shittlerton. Final ms. Missing.

Public Record Office: Hearth Tax continued

(Exemption certificates) **(County)**
1670-1 [326/7] (2,500); **1672** [326/12] (250) (not mentioned in D.R.S.7); **1673-4** [326/8] (500). Paper, some on printed forms, 84 in 326/7, allocated to hds. in D.R.S. **7**, 46 in 326/8. Each lot bound together. Do not add any names to 1670 return [DC 9953-6].

Subsidy
1664/5. Repton and Gresley hd. [94/377] (130). Also 12 certs. of residence.

Association Oath Rolls, 1695-6 [C.213]
[66] County; [67] Derby town.

Derby Central Library (Derbyshire Collection)

Hearth Tax (originals)
1670. County (Appletree, Repton and Gresley hds missing). Paper books, originally the collectors' records. Complete and in good condition. Published, D.R.S. **7**.
Wirksworth hd. [DC 9953].
Scarsdale hd. [DC 9954].
High Peak hd. [DC 9955].
Morleston and Litchurch hd. [DC 9956].
(microfilms) **1662M. Repton and Gresley hd.** [P.R.O. E.179/245/7]. Published.
1664L. Appletree hd. [P.R.O. E.179/94/405]. Published.

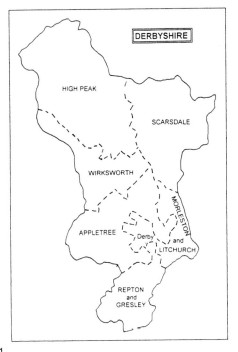

DERBYSHIRE

HIGH PEAK

SCARSDALE

WIRKSWORTH

MORLESTON

APPLETREE
Derby
and
LITCHURCH

REPTON
and
GRESLEY

21

Derbyshire continued

Various Tax Papers for **Wirksworth hd.** and parishes (including Ashbourne) within the hundred [Chandos-Pole-Gell papers, D258]

1679,1680: assessments for disbanding the army [6/12, S/6].

1677-78: parish assessments for money to build 30 war ships [28/6, 33; 29/13; 56/40].

1673-74: assessments for his majesty's extraordinary occasions [24/11: 58/29; S/5].

1678, 1689: *Poll Tax,* Wirksworth wapentake [56/41; 48/10].

1693. Assessment of the constablery of Dethick, Tansley and Lea for a tax for carrying on a vigorous war against France [1088 M/R 19].

1705-1719: occasional *Land Tax* assessments for parishes within wapentake.

17th century (unspecified): other assessments, not been possible to tie to individual taxes.

Marriage Tax, **1696, 1698:** Tibshelf [D1091A/PO2].
Window Tax, **1713-14:** Hathersage [D1970A].

Free and Voluntary Present, **1661-2**
Scarsdale hd. [DD.3P 2/1]. List of subscribers taken at Alfreton, Bolsover, Dronfield and Chesterfield. 8ms.
High Peak hd. [DD.3P 2/2]. List of subscribers taken at Bakewell, Tideswell and Chapel en le Frith. 4ms.

Marriage Tax, **1696, Darley** [Bar D.728] (250). Copy CAMPOP.

DEVON

Note: Exeter assessed separately from the County.

Publications

Devon Hearth Tax Return: Lady Day 1674, ed. and pub. T.L. Stoate, 1982. Full transcript of **1674L** [P.R.O. E.179/245/17] (22,919). Also includes an index to places in the 1664L return [E.179/102/530]; introduction discusses and analyses extant records of the Hearth Tax for the county. Indexed.

Exeter in the Seventeenth Century: Tax and Rate Assessments, 1602-1699, ed. W.G. Hoskins, Devon and Cornwall Record Society, N.S., vol. 2, 1957, includes *Poll Tax,* **1660** [Exeter City Archives, Box 4; P.R.O. duplicate, E.179/102/482] (6,845); Hearth Tax, **1671M** [Exeter City Archives Misc. Rolls No. 74; P.R.O. duplicate E.179/102/534] (2,400). Indexed.

Free and Voluntary Present, **1661-2**

North Tawton hd. [102/519] (159). Flat, fading in parts.

Hearth Tax (Assessments and returns)
(those available on microfilm from P.R.O. marked §: copies are in the *West Country Studies Library, Exeter Central Library*).

1662M. Exeter city [102/520] (800). Poor condition and legibility.
  Coleridge hd. (part of Charleton Slapton, fragment of Chivelstone), **Roborough hd.** (part of Vaulterhome tithing, part of Weston Peverel), **Cliston hd.** (part of ?Broad Clyst, Butterleigh, part of Whimple) [375/13 §] (140). Fragmentary remains of County assessment.
1664L. County [102/530 §] (?4,000) Ts intro. and contents. 37 out of 150 ms. remaining. Much decayed, repaired, much illegible, but parts OK. Key to parishes in *Devon Hearth Tax 1674.*
1671M. Exeter city [102/534]. Duplicate at Devon R.O., *published* in *Exeter in the 17th Century.*
1672M-1673L. Tiverton town and parish [245/19 §] (320).
1674L. County [245/17]. *Published.*
(Arrears)
1662M. Rackenford, Fremington, Stokenham, and the hds. of Cliston, Axminster and Colyton [371/1] (11). Constables' names only. Latin.
  County [E.199/9/35]. Fairly extensive return giving arrears of persons by hundreds and parishes.

Subsidies
1663. North Tawton, Witheridge [102/489] (350). First m. badly faded and largely illegible, remainder legible.
  Same hds. [102/523] (500). Parts badly decayed or faded, but parts adequate condition and legibility.

Devon: Public Record Office: Subsidies contd,

1663 ctd. **Black Torrington hd.** [102/543] (40).
Repaired, but some decay, poor legibility.
Shebbear, Hartland hds. [245/15] (500). Repaired.
some loss from decay.
Halberton, Hayridge, Tiverton, Bampton hds.
[102/517] (250). Some decay, repaired. Part
adequately legible, but much faded or decayed:
same hds. plus Hemyock [102/524] (1,000).
Lifton hd. [102/521] (60). Repaired but much lost
through decay; legibility variable.
Stanborough hd. [102/522] (250). VG.
Plympton, Ermington hds. [245/16] (400).

Poll Tax
Note. Dr Tom Arkell, who has made a special study
of the Poll Tax, considers that some or all of these
may not be Poll Tax records. The Devon section of
the P.R.O. calendar has been revised in modern
times, and they are described as such in that.

1660. Axminster, Colyton hds. [245/14/4] (2,300).
Repaired. Great loss from decay.
Exeter city [102/482]. published in *Exeter in the
Seventeenth Century*. St. Mary de Grad (140) has
been discovered since publication.
Defaulters [102/554] (300), paper, in good
condition, good legibility.
Exminster hd. [245/14/3] (4,000). Paper book,
repaired: Bishopsteignton [278/48] (200), paper,
poor condition; Dawlish [272/45] (60), paper,
repaired; Ide [272/47] (100), paper; Kenn [272/43]
(250), poor condition. Mamhead [272/46] (75);
Powderham [369/22] (100), poor condition, variable
legibility, West Teignmouth [272/42] (300),
repaired; certificates of defaulters [102/555] (50),
repaired, bound as book, easy to use, few names.

Public Record Office: Poll Tax 1660 continued

Plympton hd. [102/481] (1,500), repaired but some
decay, legibility variable.
Wonford hd. [245/14/1] (1,000). Repaired,
considerable loss from decay. [245/14/2] (4,000).
Paper book, repaired, great loss from decay. Incl.
Dunsford, Wonford St. Thomas the Apostle,
Topsham, Whitstone; pauper East Quarter
Exeter; Tedburn St. Mary [102/518b] (250), paper
book, lower half decayed and missing, but
excellent in surviving part - listing all inhabitants
over 16. Upton Pyne [272/39]. Unfit for production.
Defaulters (also Wonford West hd) [102/552]
(?50). Paper. Well repaired, bound as book, easy
to use but few names.

Association Oath Rolls, 1695-6 [C.213]

[68-71] **County**; [72-74] **Exeter**; [75] **Totnes**;
[76-78] **Plymouth**; [79] **Okehampton**;
[80] **Barnstaple**; [81] **Plympton**; [82] **Honiton**;
[83] **Ashburton**; [84] **Dartmouth**; [85] **'Beralston'**
(? Belstone); [86] **Tiverton**; [87] **Great Torrington**;
[88] **Crediton**; [89] **Bideford**; [90] **Ottery St.Mary**;
[91] **South Molton**; [92] **Topsham**.

Devon Record Office, *Exeter*

Hearth Tax

1662M. Constables' original lists for **Crediton hd.**:
Colebrook, Crediton, Kennerleigh, Morchard
Bishop, Sandford; **Exminster hd.**: Ashcombe,
Ashton, Chudleigh, Dawlish, Diddiscombe,
Dunchideock, Exminster, Ide, Kenn, Mamhead,
Powderham, Shillingford, East and West
Teignmouth; **Plympton hd.**: Brixton, Plymstock,
Revelstoke, Shaugh, Wembury, Yealmpton;
Stanborough hd.: West Alvington, Buckfast-
leigh, Churchstow, Dean Prior, Holne, North
Huish, Moreleigh, Rattery; **Tavistock hd.**:
Brentor, Milton Abbot, Tavistock.

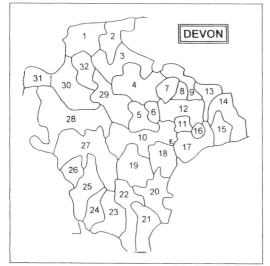

Key to Map of Devon Hundreds		
14	Axminster	20	Haytor
9	Bampton	13	Hemyock
28	Black Torrington	27	Lifton
1	Braunton	3	South Molton
17	East Budleigh	16	Ottery St. Mary
6	West Budleigh	24	Plympton
11	Cliston	25	Roborough
21	Coleridge	30	Shebbear
15	Colyton	2	Shirwell
5	Crediton	22	Stanborough
23	Ermington	26	Tavistock
E	Exeter	29	North Tawton
18	Exminster		and Winkleigh
32	Fremington	19	Teignbridge
8	Halberton	7	Tiverton
31	Hartland	4	Witheridge
12	Hayridge	10	Wonford

Devon: *Devon Record Office, Hearth Tax* contd.

Exeter city muniments: **1671M, 1672M, 1673L, 1674L.** The first is published in *Exeter in the Seventeenth Century.*

Association Oath Roll, 1696
County [Devon Q/S20/1].

Window Tax
1710. Cadbury, Cadeleigh and Netherexe [326 M/Z 2-4]; Halberton [1160M/Parish/General/4].

Microfilm of all P.R.O. *Hearth Tax* holdings. Transcript of *Hearth Tax* **1671-74**, for **Exeter**, as in City Muniments, in collection of *Devon and Cornwall Record Society* (temporary membership available on the spot).

British Library Manuscripts Collection

Marriage Tax, **1698:** Buckfastleigh, Ringmore [BM. HARL.6832]. Copies CAMPOP.

DORSET

Publication

Hearth Tax, **1664M,** in *Dorset Hearth Tax Assessments 1662-64* [Bodleian Library, Oxford, Rawlinson MSS. B.292-296], pub. Dorset Natural Hist. & Arch.Soc., 1951. **County** for **1664M** (11,500 names) based on and little different from 1663M. Excludes county borough of Poole. Indexed. Introduction by C.A.F. Meekings describes P.R.O. documents.

Dorset continued

Public Record Office [E.179]

Hearth Tax *(Assessments and returns)*

1663M/1664L. County [245/25]. Constables' returns, paper, bound into three books of 272ff (too much variation to estimate number of names). Includes exempt.
1673L. County [105/342a] (?). Badly decayed and most names lost, though numbers of hearths survive. Analysed in published volume, left, Appendix 7.
1673. Poole [245/26] (?100). Badly decayed, repaired, but little legible.
1674L. County [105/346] (?). Much decayed though repaired. Faded and mainly illegible.
(Exemption certificates)
1671-74 [327/1] (many). Unarranged printed forms, no obvious order.

Poll Tax (?)
1661-2. Poole [245/24] (450). Paper; variable legibility. Arranged alphabetically (initial letter) by landlord: tenants and some streets given.

Benevolence Money *(Free and Voluntary Gift?)*
(1661?). Sutton Waldron [245/23] (24). Paper.

Association Oath Rolls, 1695-6 [C.213]
[93-94] **County;** [95-96] **Poole;** [97] **Dorchester;** [98] **Lyme Regis;** [99] **Weymouth;** [100] **Bridport;** [101] **Shaftesbury;** [102] **Wareham;** [103] **Corfe Castle;** [104] **Bere Regis.**

Bodleian Library, *Oxford*

Hearth Tax *(Assessment)*
1664M. County (11,500). Published. [Rawlinson MSS.B.292-296: Dorchester, B.293; Shaftesbury (Shaston), B.296; Sherbourne, B.292; Blandford, B.294; Bridport, B.295]

Dorset Record Office, *Dorchester*

Marriage Tax
Lyme Regis, 1695, 1697, 1699, 1701-3 [DC/LR/H2].
Colway tithing, *c.*1695 [DC/LR/H2]. Copies with CAMPOP.

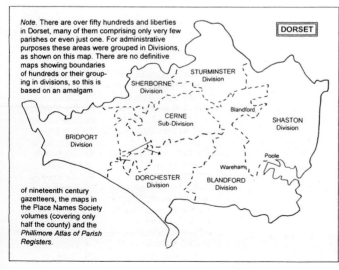

Note. There are over fifty hundreds and liberties in Dorset, many of them comprising only very few parishes or even just one. For administrative purposes these areas were grouped in Divisions, as shown on this map. There are no definitive maps showing boundaries of hundreds or their grouping in divisions, so this is based on an amalgam of nineteenth century gazetteers, the maps in the Place Names Society volumes (covering only half the county) and the *Phillimore Atlas of Parish Registers.*

DORSET

STURMINSTER Division

SHERBORNE Division

CERNE Sub-Division

Blandford

SHASTON Division

BRIDPORT Division

Poole

Wareham

DORCHESTER Division

BLANDFORD Division

Co. DURHAM

Note. Norhamshire, Islandshire and Bedlingtonshire, now in Northumberland, are included in Co. Durham records. For Berwick see under Northumberland.

Publication

'The Hearth Tax', *J. Nhumbd. & Durham FHS*, **3**, 3 (Aug 1978), pp. 88-89, gives details of Northumberland and Durham records at the P.R.O. and elsewhere.

Public Record Office [E.179]

Hearth Tax (Assessments and returns).
(those available on microfilm from P.R.O. marked §; asterisked items are also at *Durham County R.O.*).

1662M. County [106/20 §] (1,200).
1663L. County [106/21 §]* (1,200).
1664L. County [106/27 §]* (8,000). Parts decayed or faded, but mostly legible.
1665M. County [245/27 §]* (7,500). Exempt not shown. Includes Bedlingtonshire, Norhamshire and Holy Island.
1666L. County [106/28 §]* (13,900). VG, paper ms., stitched at top, flat, easy to use. Contents list of wards. Includes Bedlingtonshire, Norhamshire and Holy Island.
1670M. County [106/26 §] (?1,000). Poor condition, repaired and legibilty. Introduction and contents list.
1671M? County [375/5 §]* (250). Variations since 1670M. Includes Bedlingtonshire, Norhamshire and Holy Island.
1674L. County [106/25 §]* (14,200). Includes Bedlingtonshire, Norhamshire and Holy Island.
(? yr). Durham [244/38] (12). Fragment, Chester ward, west division of Whickham.
Durham[245/28 §] (100). Bad legibility. Not clear if Hearth Tax at all.

Co. Durham: *Public Record Office* continued

Hearth Tax (Arrears)
1662M. County [106/22]*(2,000). Desperate.
1662M-1663L. County [106/23]*(500).
1666L. County [106/24]*(1,250). Flat parchment sheets. Includes Bedlingtonshire, Norhamshire and Holy Island.

Association Oath Rolls, **1695-6** [C.213] [105] County; [106] Durham city.

Durham County Record Office, Durham

Microfilm of P.R.O. held *Hearth Tax* records asterisked above.

ESSEX

Publications

1662M. County, surname only indexed, microfiche published by Society of Genealogists, 1990.
Analysis of *Hearth Tax* returns for **Ongar hd.**, *V.C.H. Essex*, **4**, 1956, pp. 303-10, by K.H. Burley.

Index

Hearth Tax, **1662M** [Essex Record Office Q/RTh 1] (20,000). For all parishes; poor persons excluded.

Public Record Office [E.179]

Free and Voluntary Present, **1661-2**
County [246/7] (3,000). Occupations given.

Hearth Tax (Assessments and returns)
(those available on microfilm from P.R.O. marked §; copies of HT rolls 1662-75 are in *Essex Record Office* [T/A 169]).

1662M. County [246/8 §] (5,000). Badly decayed but repaired. Much lost from decay and surviving ms. often faded.
Barking and **Woodham Ferris** [246/9 §] (250). Paper.
Danbury [246/10 §] (70). Paper, poor condition.
Margaretting, Liston (exempt), H--ing [358]. Constables' stray returns.
1664M. Dengie hd. [246/25 §] (2,000). Paper book, annotated. VG.
Freshwell hd. [246/14 §] (600). Annotated paper book. VG.
Hinckford hd. [246/26 §] (2,500). Paper book. VG.
Hinckford hd. [112/687] (2,400). Paper book, annotated. VG.
Uttlesford and **Clavering hds.** [246/13] (4,000). Annotated paper book. VG.
Uttlesford and **Clavering hds.** [246/28] (1,500). Paper book, VG.
Uttlesford, Freshwell, Clavering hds. [246/27 §] (2,250). Paper book, VG.

Essex: *Public Record Office, Hearth Tax* contd.

1665L. Uttlesford, Freshwell and **Clavering hds.**
[246/17 §] (2,500). Annotated paper book, VG.
1665M. Uttlesford, Freshwell, Clavering hds.
[246/16 §] (2,000); **Winstree hd.** [246/18] (1,000).
Annotated paper books.
(1665). Lexden hd. [246/15 §] (4,000). Paper book,
annotated. VG.
1666L. Becontree hd. [246/24 §] (1,200).
Annotated paper book. VG.
1666M. Uttlesford, Freshwell, Dunmow,
Tendring, Hinckford, Winstree, Lexden hds.
and **Colchester** [246/20 §] (10,000). Annotated
paper book, VG.
(1666). Harlow, Waltham, Witham, Chelmsford,
Clavering, Chafford, Barstable, Ongar hds.,
Havering liberty [246/19 §] (9,000). Annotated
paper book, VG.
(1666?). Rochford hd. [246/21] (2,000). Annotated
paper book, VG.
(1673). County [246/12 §] (5,000). Badly decayed
but repaired. Much lost from decay, but legible
when surviving.
(1675). County. [246/22] (12,000).
(? yr.). Haverhill and Wethersfield [246/29 §] (150).

Essex: *Public Record Office* continued

Subsidies
1663. Barstable and **Chafford hds.** [112/694]
(400).
Chelmsford hd. [112/695] (300).
Colchester [112/692]. Badly decayed.
Dengie hd. [112/693] (93). Flat sheets.
Ongar hd. [112/696] (100). Badly torn, faded but
legible.
Uttlesford and **Clavering hds.** [112/691] (400).
Most legible, parts badly worn.
(1664). Ongar, Harlow, Waltham [112/697] (?300).
Very badly decayed, repaired. Legibility adequate
when not lost.
Uttlesford and **Clavering hds.** [112/615a] (100).
Much lost from decay, repaired.
(? yr.). Barfield Saling and Magna, some other
places [246/29] (500).

Association Oath Rolls, **1695-6** [C.213]
[107] **County;** [108] **Colchester;** [473] **Colchester**
Quakers; [109-10] **Maldon;** [111] **Saffron Walden;**
[112] **Harwich.**

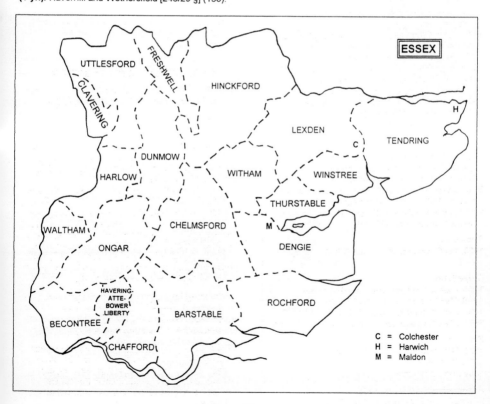

Essex continued

All *Hearth Tax* holdings of the P.R.O. are on microfilm at E.R.O. [T/A 169].
There is an **Index** to the 1662M Hearth Tax [E.R.O. Q/RTh 1] (20,000) for all parishes, poor persons excluded. See also *publications*.

Hearth Tax (see *Guide to the Essex Record Office*, F.G. Emmison, 1969, page 29).

1662M. County [Q/RTh 1] (20,000). Enrolment of returns. Complete for every parish and constablewick; excluded exempt poor. **Indexed.**

1668(?). [Q/RTh 2]. Poor persons and house-holders having an increase or decrease in hearths since 1663. Original returns by constables and collectors. One bundle for Hds. of Chelmsford, Clavering, Dunmow, Freshwell, Hinckford, Lexden, Tendring and Uttlesford, and liberty of Havering and town of Colchester. [Q/RTh 3-4]. Enrolment of returns of increases and decreases in hearths since ?1663. Two rolls. Same Hds. as in Q/RTh 2.

1670M(?). County [Q/RTh 5] (29,300). Enrolment. Complete. Includes exempt and number of poor receiving alms, un-named.

1672 (July). **County** [Q/RTh 6]. Original returns of increases and decreases in hearths. Complete. Also includes new householders.
County [Q/RTh 7]. Enrolment of Q/RTh 6.
(c.1673). [Q/RTh 9]. Copies of returns. (seven booklets). Incomplete; for hds. of Becontree, Clavering, Dunmow, Lexden, Tendring and Witham, liberty of Havering and town of Colchester. Names differ only slightly from same Hds. in Q/RTh 8. This may be a fair copy.

1674L?. [Q/RTh 8]. Copies of returns (15 booklets); complete except for Hds. of Barstable, Becontree (part), Chafford, Clavering, Harlow and Liberty of Havering. Includes exempt poor.
Newport parish book [D/P 15/8/1] includes lists of hearths 1662, 1663; and exemptions 1668, 1671.
Wormingford register [D/P 185/1/1] includes list of persons exempt from HT 1668.

Subsidies
1663, 1664, Becontree Half hd. [D/DCv 1, ff.4-5, 7-8].

(Royal) Aid
1664-5. Becontree Hd. and **Havering Liberty** [D/DMs 023/1-21; D/DMy 15M50/670, 671].
1689. Havering Liberty [D/DMs 025/1-4].
1664-1704. Newport parish book [D/P 15/8/1].

Poll Tax
1690. Great Dunmow: Bigods Quarter [D/DB 1112].
Newport parish book [D/P 15/8/1].

Association Oath Rolls, 1696
57 parishes, *c.*2,000 names [Q/RRO 2].

Essex continued

Land Tax
1698. Becontree and **Chafford hds.**, **Havering Liberty** [D/DMs 027/1-28].

Marriage Tax
Little Parndon, 1695, 1697, 1699 [D/P 34/1/2].

Window Tax
Maldon borough [D/B 3/3/412].

Other assessments, rates, etc.
Great Dunmow: Bigod's Quarter, monthly assessment, 1669 [D/DB 1109]; assessment, 1671 [D/DB 1110]; tax for disbanding the army 1679/80 [D/DB 1111].
Little Sampford: vestry book includes tax assessments, 1667-1704 [D/P 122/8/1].
Writtle: rate, 1667 [D/DP 07/6].

GLOUCESTERSHIRE and BRISTOL

Note: Bristol was assessed separately. Gloucester was assessed separately from Gloucestershire.

Publications

'The *Hearth Tax* in Bristol, and 'Bristol *Tax Assessments* in the Later Stuart Period (1660-1715)', both by J.S.W. Gibson, *Jnl of Bristol and Avon FHS*, **36, 37**, describe the various tax lists in the Bristol Record Office.
*The Inhabitants of **Bristol** in 1696*, Elizabeth Ralph and Mary Williams, Bristol Record Society, vol. **25**, 1968, from the Tax on marriages, births and burials, bachelors and widowers. The original records, complete for all 18 Bristol parishes, are in the Bristol Record Office (12,800 names). Indexed.
Hearth Tax: Olveston (Glos.), 1671 [from G.R.O. photocopy] (60), including Upper Tockington, *Jnl of Bristol and Avon FHS*, 26 (Winter 1981).

Hearth Tax (Assessments and returns)
(those available on microfilm from P.R.O. marked §)

1662M. County [116/554 §] (7.500). Fair copy. Part entirely lost, part repaired, reasonable condition and legibility. Introduction and contents list of hds.
Bristol [247/11 §] (1,600). In Latin. Parchment sheets, some dingy, but repaired. Good when not decayed.

27

1664L. County [247/16 §] (?15-20,000). Detailed contents list with each hd. in separate bound sections. Much decay and poor legibility. Introductions give number of hearths.

 Bristol [375/16] (600). Very badly decayed and much also illegible from fading. Short ms., repaired and sewn at top. Detailed introduction.

1671L. Bristol [116/541 §] (3,000). Includes exempt poor.

1671L-1672L. County [247/13 §] (15-20,000). Badly decayed, repaired. Mostly good legibility when not lost from decay. Introduction and contents lists of hds.

1672M. County [247/14 §] (20,000). Decayed and faded in parts, but much OK. Introduction and contents of hds. (two volume photostat copy at *Gloucestershire Record Office.*).

1673L. Bristol [247/15 §] (?3,000). Very badly decayed. Ms. Stitched head to foot. Not much examined, but mostly illegible. Modern contents list and introduction; similar to 1671L 116/541.

(Exemption certificates).

1672-3. County [116/544 §] (5,000). Loose paper sheets, easy to use.

(Arrears - hopeful)

1663L. Gloucester (city) [116/539 §] (200).

GLOUCESTERSHIRE and BRISTOL

B	= Berkeley (detached)
G	= Gloucester
DofL	= Duchy of Lancaster
LB	= Lower Berkeley
MD	= Middle Dudstone and King's Barton
UL&S	= Upper Langley and Swinehead
UpTew	= Upper Tewkesbury
UpTh	= Upper Thornbury
W	= Westminster

Glos. and Bristol, *Public Record Office* contd.

Subsidies

1663. Berkeley, Grumbaldsash, Langley and Swineshead, Thornbury, Henbury, Pucklechurch and **Barton Regis hds.** [247/12] (1,000).
Forest of Dean (divn) [116/538] (110). Poor condition.
Bristol [116/537] (200). Bad condition and mostly illegible.
(?1663). Bristol [116/547] (100). Poor condition, part badly faded.

Poll Tax
(1660). Kiftsgate (upper divn.) [116/535] (500). Very badly decayed, but much remains legible.

Association Oath Rolls, 1695-6 [C.213]
[113] **County;** [114] **Gloucester;**
[115] **Cirencester;** [116] **Tewkesbury;**
[117] **Tetbury;** [223-24] **Bristol.**

Gloucestershire Record Office, *Gloucester*

(Daily charge made).

Hearth Tax
1672M. County [D.383]. 2 vol. photostat copy of P.R.O. E.179/247/14
1662M and **1671-2. Kemerton** [D4614/16]. Photocopies of P.R.O. E.179/116/554 and E.179/247/14.
1662. Alderley [D1086/R2]. Constables' book. Original return of hearths assessed for poor rate.
1674. Cirencester St. John Baptist [P86a CW2/1]. Churchwardens' accounts: List of persons exempt.
1686. Westbury-on-Severn [P354 CO 1/2].

Subsidies, Aids etc.
Westbury-on-Severn [P354 CO 1/2]: 1664/5; 1666; 1668; 1671; 1677; 1692/3.
Swindon, 1677 [D 2375/X1].

Poll Tax
1678, Deerhurst, Cleeve and **Lower Westminster hds.** [D5555/2/14].

Marriage Tax
1695, Stinchcombe [P312/MI 3].

Land Tax
1700, Shipton Moyne [D1571/E304].
c.1700, Twyning [P343 M11]
1710, Cheltenham, Cleeve and **Lower Deerhurst Hds** [D1637 X2].
1710, 1722 Stinchcombe [P312 MI/1].
1710, Woolaston [D2700/14209].
1711, Dyrham and Hinton [D1799 E168].
1713, Chedworth [Q/Rel 1b].
1714, Tidenham [D2700/14203].

Window Tax
1710, Stinchcombe [P312 MI/4].

Gloucestershire and Bristol continued

Gloucester City Library

Hearth Tax: **1672L.** Painswick [9930]. Certificate of persons exempt.
Marriage Tax: **1696.** North Nibley [Smyth of Nibley Papers, vol. 4].

Bristol Record Office, *Bristol.*

See *Guide to the Bristol Archives Office,* E. Ralph. 1971, pp 45-48.
This Office has a magnificent collection of tax assessments from 1663 on, comparable only with the City of London. Rather than separate them into different tax categories, they are shown in chronological order of assessment, following approximately the order of the published Guide. However, they are so numerous that it is not practicable to indicate the number of documents for each tax, their references nor the number of names each may include.

1663-4. Subsidy.
1665-8. Aid.
1665-73. Hearth Tax. **1671 indexed.**
1666-7. Poll Tax, maintenence of war.
1667-8. Additional Aid.
1671. Subsidy, supply of extraordinary occasions.
1673-4. Supply of extraordinary occasions.
1677-8. Thirty ships of war.
1678. Poll Tax, war with France.
1679-80. Supply for disbanding the army.
1679-80. Further supply for disbanding the army.
1689. Aid.
1689. Poll Tax, reduction of Ireland.
1689. Aid, defence of the realm.
1689-90. Aid.
1689-90. Poll and Additional Poll Tax for reduction of Ireland.
1690. Poll Tax, reduction of Ireland and war with France.
1691-3. Aid (Land Tax), war with France
1692-3. Poll Tax, war with France.
1693-5. Aid, war with France.
1694-5. Poll Tax, war with France.
1695-1706. Tax on marriages, births and burials, bachelors and widowers, war against France. 1696 (complete for the 18 parishes). *Published.* see page 27.
1696-1707. Aid, war with France.
1696. Window Tax.
1699-1808. Several rates or duties on houses: Houses; Windows and Lights Tax.
1698-9. Disbanding the forces.
1698. Quarterly Poll Tax.
1699. Disbanding the army.
1701. Defraying expenses of Navy, Guards and Garrisons.
1702-1849. Aid and Land Tax.
1703. Subsidies, war against France and Spain.
1696-1798. Land Tax.

29

HAMPSHIRE and ISLE OF WIGHT

Note: Southampton was assessed separately from the County.

Publications

The Hampshire Hearth Tax Assessment, 1665 [P.R.O. E.179/176/565] (23,150), *with the Southampton Assessments for 1662* [Southampton C.R.O. SC14/2/32b] *and 1670* [P.R.O. 179/247/29], ed. Elizabeth Hughes and Philippa White, Hampshire Record Series 11 (Hants. C.C.), 1992. Indexed. The Isle of Wight is omitted.
Hearth Tax Returns for the Isle of Wight, 1664 to 1674, ed. P.D.D. Russell, Isle of Wight County Record Office, 1981. Indexed. This includes **all** HT records relating to the Isle of Wight from the various P.R.O. E.179 documents listed below. Very detailed introduction with description of all records. Appendix lists Isle of Wight arrears 1669-73.

Public Record Office [E.179].

Free and Voluntary Present, 1661-2
County [176/559] (?4,000). Parchment roll, ms. stitched head to foot. Very long and unwieldy, good condition and legibility. Ts transcript of IoW at *IoW R.O.*
Southampton [176/571] (150). Bad condition.

Hearth Tax *(Assessments and returns)*
(those available on microfilm from P.R.O. marked §; County 1665L and all IoW records *published;* photocopies of Winchester lists in *Hampshire R.O.*)

1664L. County [375/32] (17,700). Basingstoke, Kingsclere, Isle of Wight and Alton divns., some losses; Fawley ?Soke) and New Forest divns., considerable losses; Andover and Portsdown divns., little remains.
1664 March/June. **County** [176/564] (6,000). Miscellaneous paper returns, bound. Introduction and contents list. Easy to use, though poor handwriting.
1665L. County [176/565 §]. Shows exempt poor. New Forest annotated, increases and decreases. Microfilm at Hampshire Record Office. *Published.*
1670M. Southampton [247/29] (500). Flattened parchment sheets, easy to use. *Published.*
1673L. County [176/569] (20,000). Repaired but some loss from decay to lower parts of ms.
1674L. County [247/30] (24,000). Poor condition and faded, but better than 176/569. Contents list of parishes.
(Exemption certificates)
1670-1. County [176/568] (5,000). Paper, mainly printed, bound in two books.
1672-3. County [330/1].
1673-4. County [176/570] (4,000). Loose folded paper sheets, no special order.
(Arrears)
See Isle of Wight *published* volume.

Hampshire, *Public Record Office,* continued

Subsidies
1663 May. **Alton division** [247/26] (450). Marked 'unfit for production' but in fact in adequate preservation.
1663 Oct. **Alton division** [175/540] (400).
1663 Nov. **Fawley hd.** [176/560] (65). Bad condition.
(1663). Soke of Winchester [176/563] (500). Bad condition and legibility.
1663/4 March. **Kingsclere division** [176/561] (400). **Portsdown division** [247/28] (500).
(1664) Basingstoke division [247/27] (500). Repaired. Some loss from decay.
Isle of Wight [176/562] (200).
No date. Portsdown [176/581] (150). Bad fading and staining in part.
Barton Stacey hd. [176/583] (60). Bad condition. Incl. Nuton Stacey, Sutton Scotney, Priors Dean and Colmere, Headbourne Worthy.

Poll Tax
(1660). Evingar, Kingsclere hds. [176/558] (500). Very bad condition.

Association Oath Rolls, 1695-6 [C.213].
[240] **County** (incl. Winchester);
[241] **Southampton** [242-3] **Portsmouth;**
[244] **Portsmouth Dockyard;** [245] **Yarmouth;**
[246] **Petersfield;** [247] **Newport;**
[248] **Stockbridge;** [249] **Christchurch;**
[250] **Lymington;** [251] **Whitchurch;**
[252] **Andover;** [253] **Basingstoke;** [254] **Romsey;**
[255] **Gosport;** [256] **Isle of Wight.**

Hampshire Record Office, *Winchester.*

Hearth Tax
1665L. County [microfilm of P.R.O. E.179/176/565]. *Published.*
Photocopies of **Winchester** P.R.O. E.179:
1664. The City, The Soke and Milland [176/564].
1665L. The City, The Soke, Milland, Alton, Fawley. Chilcombe, Avington, Sparkford and Weeke [176/565].
1670. Exemption certificates [176/568].
1673. The City, The Soke, St. Peter Chesil, Avington, Chilcombe, Weeke, Winnall, Sparkford (parts)(also exemption certificates) [176/569,570].
1674. The City, The Soke, St. Maurice, St. John, St. Peter Chesil [247/30].
also
1663. Michelmersh [from Dorset Hearth Tax returns: Photocopy 69].

30

Hampshire Record Office continued

Poll Tax
1689. Hurn and Parley [7M54/264].
1699. East Woodhay [Photocopy 362 of original in
Berkshire Record Office].

Miscellaneous
Hurn and Parley (premises in). Receipt book of
Edward Hooper for payments for Hearth Tax,
Window Tax, Land Tax, Royal Aids, Subsidies,
parish rates, etc., 1664-78, 1701-50, 1753-5
[7M54/264].
Hurn and East Parley, Royal Aid, 1665, 1691
[7M54/262].

Window Tax
1714. Headbourne Worthy [27M60/L11].

Land Tax
Binsted. 1689, 1691-3, 1698, 1701, 1704, 1710
[3M51/537-543].
West Boarhunt. 1703, 1704, 1715 [5M50/1254-
1261].
Portchester. 1707 [5M50/1420].
Southwick. 1710, 1712, 1715 [5M50/1848-1850].
Wymering. 1704, 1705, 1712 [5M50/1949-1952].

| **Isle of Wight Record Office,** Newport |

Ts transcript of IoW portion of *Free and Voluntary
Present 1661*, P. Russell [P.R.O. E.179/176/559].

Hampshire continued

| **Southampton Civic Record Office** |

Free and Voluntary Present, **1661-2**
Southampton, all wards [SC/14/2/32a].

Hearth Tax
1662M. All wards [SC/14/2/32b]. *Published.*

Assessments for Aids and Subsidies [all refs.
preceded by SC/14/2/]
1664-5, 1668, 1674; 1689; 1691; 1692: All wards
[33-6; 39-42a; 43-4; 45-7].
1693. St. Lawrence [54].
1694; 1697-8: All wards [55-61; 83-8, 97]
1699. All wards except Holy Rood [98-103].

Poll Tax [all refs. SC/14/2/]
*c.***1678.** All Saints [37b].
1678. St. John (incomplete) [38].
1678, 1689. Holy Rood [42b].
1692, 1697. All wards [48-54; 89-94].
1698. All Saints Infra and Extra [95-96].
1699. All wards except St. Mary [104-10].

Marriage Tax
1695-97. All parishes (some incomplete for 1695)
[SC/14/2/62-82]. Indexed.

**Hundreds and Liberties
constituting Divisions**

Alton: Alton, Finchdean, East
Meon, Selborne, Bishop's Sutton.
Andover: Andover, Barton Stacey,
King's Somborne, Thorngate,
Wherwell.
Basingstoke: Basingstoke, Bentley
Lib., Bermondspit, Crondall,
Holdshot, Micheldever, Odiham.
Kingsclere: Chuteley, Evingar,
Kingsclere, Overton, Pastrow.
New Forest: Beaulieu Lib.,
Breamore Lib., Christchurch,
Dibden Lib., Fordingbridge, New
Forest, Redbridge, Ringwood,
Westover Lib.
Portsdown: Alverstoke Lib.,
Bosmere, Fareham, Hambledon,
Havant Lib., Meonstoke,
Portsdown, Portsmouth and
Portsea Island Lib., Titchfield,
Bishop's Waltham.
Southampton town.
Isle of Wight: East and West
Medina.
City of Winchester.
Soke of Winchester:
Bountisborough, Buddlesgate,
Fawley. Mainsborough.
Mainsbridge.

HAMPSHIRE

KINGSCLERE
Division

BASINGSTOKE
Division

ANDOVER
Division

W

ALTON
Division

SOKE of WINCHESTER

S

NEW FOREST Division

PORTSDOWN
Division

EAST

WEST

P

ISLE of WIGHT
Division

P = Portsmouth
S = Southampton
W = Winchester

HEREFORDSHIRE

Publications

'The *Hearth Tax* in Herefordshire' by M.A. Faraday, *Transactions of the Woolhope Naturalists' Field Club, Herefs.*, vol. 41, 1973, Pt.1, pp.77-90. Returns described and compared, but no names, statistical table of totals only. Totals for 1662M, 1664L, 1664M, 1666L, 1671M below taken from this article.

'The *Hearth Tax*', by John Harnden, *Herefs FHS Jnl* 2 8 (Winter 85), pp. 335-8.

Public Record Office [E.179]

Free and Voluntary Present, 1661-2

County [248/11] (3,000). Rolls, badly decayed at foot, repaired and flattened. Parts illegible through decay, otherwise in good legible condition.

Hearth Tax (Assessments and returns)

(those available on microfilm from P.R.O. marked §)

1662M. County [119/482] (8,092). Poor legibility on earlier ms. but OK for most.
1664L. County [119/492 §] (13,008). Exempt poor included. Mf and transcript at *H.R.O.*
1664M. County [119/485/4] (7,803).
1665L. County [119/485/3] (7,600). Annotated.
1665M. County [119/486] (7,600). VG. Annotated. Microfilm and indexed TS transcript at *Hereford Record Office*.
1666L. County [119/487] (?9,000). VG.
1670M. County [248/13] (?14,000). Repaired but some loss from decay and much poor legibility, though some ms. are OK.
1671M. County [248/14] (13,789). First few ms. illegible from staining or fading, but most OK. Exempt poor incl.
1673L. County [119/493] (7,800). Brief contents list by CAFM. Missing 1m. (Greytree hd.). Some decay, repaired, much faded and illegible, parts OK.

Note. Of these, Faraday states those for 1664L, 1665L and 1671M are best.

(Exemption certificates).
1662-1674 [331] (very many). Two boxes.
1. Flat, paper certificates.
2. Bag, with paper certificates in rolls, some printed. Also includes Herts. and Hunts.

(Arrears)
1671. County [358].

Subsidies
1662/3. Radlow hd. [248/12] (150).
  Wigmore hd. [119/484] (211). 4ms., sewn head to foot.
(1664). Wigmore hd. [237/45] (227).

Public Record Office continued

Poll Tax

1678. County [119/491] (?,300). Collectors' names only, except for short lists of defaulters for Leominster and Lydley.
  Leominster [237/46] (300). Paper. VG. Arranged by ward. Transcript at *Hereford Record Office*.

Association Oath Rolls, 1695-6 [C.213]
[118] **County**; [119] **Hereford**; [120] **Leominster.**

County Record Office
(Hereford and Worcester C.C.), Hereford.

Mfs of *Hearth Tax* **1664L** and **1665M, County** [P.R.O. E/179/119/492 & 486]. Indexed TS transcripts (also at *Society of Genealogists*).
Transcripts of *Army Disbandment Tax*, **1678, Leominster** [P.R.O. E.179/237/46], by Michael Faraday.

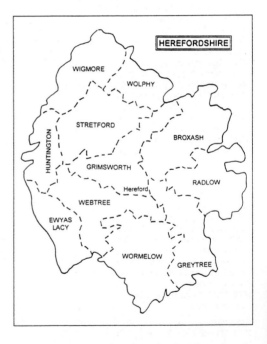

HERTFORDSHIRE

Publications

Publication of *Hearth Tax* for the **County** **1663L&M** [P.R.O. E.179/248/23,24] and **Braughing** hd. **1665L&M** [E.179/248/27], already transcribed, is envisaged by Herts. FPHS.

Public Record Office [E.179]

Hearth Tax (Assessments and returns).
(those available on microfilm from P.R.O. marked §; copies at *Hertfordshire R.O.*).

1662M. County [375/30 §] (?5,000). Introduction and parish contents list by CAFM. Very variable, some excellent.

1663L. County [248/23 §] (many). Constables' returns. Loose paper sheets, repaired, in no special order. Contents list.

1663M. County [248/24 §] (many). Constables' returns. Cashio hd. missing. Paper sheets, arranged by hd., repaired and guarded. Introduction by CAFM.

1664M-1665M. Braughing hd.
[248/27 §] (1,400). Paper book. Some pages torn, but usable.

1666L. Sub-collectors' sworn statements. Paper lists for Cheshunt, Rickmansworth, Sarratt, Abbots Langley, Hemel Hempstead, Tring, Frithsden, Northchurch, Great Gaddesden, Watford, Cashio, Oxhey only [248/25 §] (350).

Hertford and **Braughing hds.**
[248/28 §] (850). Collectors' paper book. VG.

(1666L). Hertford hd. [248/28] (150). Collector's paper book. Includes St. John's Wormley, St. Margaret's Amwell. Shows exempt poor, etc.

1670. Hitchin [121/349] (245). Paper, schedule of exemptions, by ward.

1673L. County [375/31 §] (?9,000). Introduction and contents lists of parishes by CAFM. Much decay, repaired. Legibility generally poor.
(Exemption certificates)
1670-74. [331]. As entry under Herefordshire.

Subsidies
1663. Cashio hd. [121/346] (500).
No date. Broadwater, Hitchin hds.
[121/353] (137). Torn at foot.

Association Oath Rolls, 1695 [C.213]
[121] **County;**
[122] Lord Lieutenant, etc.,
[123-24] **St. Albans;**
[125] **Hertford.**

Hertfordshire Record Office, Hertford

The *Hertfordshire Record Office* has microfilm of all P.R.O. *Hearth Tax* returns listed.

Hearth Tax
1662, 1663. Essendon, list of hearths [D/P37/8A/1]. Subsidies and Land Tax Assessments 1655-1724. Essendon [D/P37/8A/1].

Land Tax
1690. Cashio, Dacorum hds. [D/EX294 Z1].
From **1711.** Parishes in **Cashio, Hertford, Braughing, Broadwater hds.**

Association Oath Rolls, 1695-6
Bishops Stortford, Eastwick, Gilston, Sawbridgeworth, Stanstead Abbots, Thorley [QS Misc. 912-917].

Window Tax
1711-26. Essendon [D/P 37 8A/1].
1712-3. Broxbourne [LT Misc.10].

33

HUNTINGDONSHIRE

Public Record Office [E.179]

Hearth Tax *(Assessments and returns)*
(those available on microfilm from P.R.O. marked §)

1664L. County [122/227 §] (?4,000). Badly decayed and much illegible.
1664M. County [122/226 §] (6,500). Annotated.
1666L. County [249/1 §] (6,800). Paper book. Good. Transcript available, checking in progress.
1670M-1673L. County [249/4 §] (1,000). Much lost from decay, repaired. Includes part of Hurstingtone hd.
1674L. County [249/2 §] (6,800). Indexed transcript at *CRO Huntingdon* and *Cambridge*.
(Exemption certificates)
1670-74. [331]. As entry under Herefordshire.

Association Oath Rolls, 1695-6 [C.213].
[126] **Huntingdonshire**; [127] **Huntingdon**;
[128] **Godmanchester.**

County Record Office (Cambs.C.C., Huntingdon Branch), *Huntingdon*

Microfilm of P.R.O. *Hearth Tax* records E.179/ 122/226, 249/1,2,4 (also *Poll Tax* 249/3, 1692, parish totals only)

Window Tax
Stanground. 1698-1752 [2776/18/9-12].
Great Catworth, 1702 [DDM 5C/8].
Hemingford Abbots, 1709 [25537/9].

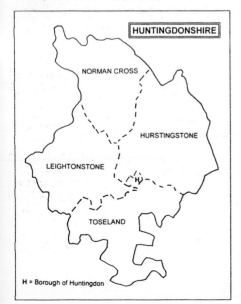

H = Borough of Huntingdon

KENT

Note: Canterbury and the Cinque Ports were assessed separately from the county.

Publications

Kent Hearth Tax Enrolled Assessment 1664L:
1. Lathe of St. Augustine [Centre for Kentish Studies Q/RTh] (3,300), ed. D.W. Harrington, Kent FHS Record Pubn. No. **14** and Microfiche **14** (£1.80), 1983. Indexed.
2. Lathe of Shepway (Romney Marsh) [Centre for Kentish Studies Q/RTh], ed. D.W. Harrington, Kent FHS Microfiche **182** (£1.50).
The whole county has been transcribed and is likely to be published eventually.
Sevenoaks Wills and Inventories in the Reign of Charles II, Kent Record Soc. **25** (1988) incl. **1664L** Hearth Tax for Sevenoaks and the Liberty of Riverhead.
Hearth Tax Returns **1664**, *Gravesend, Milton, Northfleet, Southfleet.* 8pp. 65p from E.R. Green, 49 Dennis Road, Gravesend.
Hearth Tax for the Hundred of Little and Lessness, Kent, **1662M, 1663M** [P.R.O. E.179/129/702/206, 179/249/31/13], extracted and indexed by J.E. Packer, 1983-85 (duplicated TS). Includes Crayford, Erith, East Wickham, Plumstead. Copies at *LB of Bexley LS Library, LB of Greenwich LH Dept, P.R.O., Society of Genealogists, NW Kent FHS.*

Public Record Office [E 179]

Hearth Tax *(Assessments and returns)*
(most/?all returns are available on microfilm from P.R.O.; copies, 1662-1664 are held by *Centre for Kentish Studies*).

For the four returns **1662M** to **1664L** there are returns for very many (perhaps all) divisions of one or more collections. That for **1662M** has over a hundred references; **1663L** has 58; **1663M** has 38; and **1664L** has 62. The calendar has been revised and retyped and is relatively easy to consult, though the order of the documents and places is haphazard. The documents have not been examined and no estimate of numbers can be given.
1671M. County, Canterbury and Cinque Ports [129/746] (28,000). Narrow ms. Some decay, repaired, some fading, but most OK or adequate. Introduction and contents list of hds.
1673L. County, Canterbury and Cinque ports [375/21] (2,000). 'Incomplete'. Considerable fading, slight decay, repaired. Introduction by CAFM.
(Exemption certificates)
1674L. County, Canterbury and Cinque Ports [129/747] (?2,500). Printed forms, repaired, bound as book.

Kent, *Public Record Office,* continued

Subsidies
(1661). Maidstone and Eythorne hds. [129/691]
(200); [129/697] (200).
(1663). Milton [129/713] (400).
Aylesford (lathe, south) [129/728] (41).
Maidstone, Hd of Maidstone, Lower and Upper
Half Hds. of Eythorne.
No date. **St. Augustine lathe** [249/39] (250).
Fragile.
Blackheath hd. [249/44] (100). Poor legibility.

Poll Tax
No date. **Shepway lathe** [129/752] (?300). Poor
condition, only partly legible.
St. Augustine lathe [129/753] (150). Names on
left OK, but right hand column decayed and lost.

Association Oath Rolls, 1695-6 [C.213]
[129] **County;** [130] **Canterbury;** [131] **Rochester,**
etc; [132] **Maidstone;** [133] **Queenborough;**
[134] **Sheerness;** [135] **Gravesend and Milton;**
[136] **Court of Vice-Admiralty;** [137] **Prize Office,**
Dover; [332] **Cinque Ports.**

Centre for Kentish Studies, *Maidstone*

Hearth Tax

Microfilm of P.R.O. holdings of Kent *Hearth Tax,*
1662M-1664L.
1664L. County [Q/RTh] (26,000). Enrolled
assessment, including in nearly all cases houses
exempt. Omits liberties of the Cinque Ports,
Romney Marsh and Canterbury. St. Augustine
and Shepway lathes *published;* see above, left.
Whole county transcribed and for eventual
publication. Also microfilmed.
Tenterden borough records [Te] incl. **1663-4** HT.

Centre for Kentish Studies: Hearth Tax continued

New Romney borough records [NR] incl. **1662-71**
HT; and **Lydd** HT **1670.**
Darnley MSS [U1107] include HT assessments
1662M for **St. Augustine lathe:** hds. of
Bewsborough, Bleangate, Bridge and Petham,
Cornilo, Eastry, Ringslow, Westgate and
Wingham, borough of Longport (Canterbury);
Scray lathe: Marden hd.; **Shepway lathe:**
Ashford, hds. of Aloesbridge, Newchurch.
Gordon Ward collection [U1000/10] includes
Penshurst HT returns **1663.**
Phillipps MSS [U1592] include HT returns for **Chart**
and **Longbridge hds.** c.**1662M.**

Poll Tax
New Romney. 1666, 1678, 1689, 1690, 1692,
1694, 1698 [NR/RTp 4-20].
Ramsgate. 1690 [Sa/RTp 1].

Association Oath Roll, 1695-6.
County? Subscribed at Maidstone, Canterbury,
Ashford, Greenwich and Woolwich, but only c.400
names in all.

Marriage Tax
1705. 36 parishes in Wingham Petty Div., in hds. of
Bewsborough, Cornilo, Downhamford. Eastry,
Kinghamford, Preston, Ringslow and Wingham
[Q/CTz 2] (6,000).
New Romney, 1695-1706 (every year) [NR/RTb
1-13].

Window Tax
1705-33. Wingham div., lathe of St. Augustine
(nearly every parish every year) [Q/CTw] (3,000
per year).
1707-27. Rodmersham [P307/28/2].
1711. Meopham [U1127/010/1].

KENT

Lathe of
SUTTON-
AT-HONE
Rochester
Lathe of
AYLESFORD
Maidstone
Canterbury
Lathe of
ST. AUGUSTINE
Lathe of SCRAY
Lathe of SHEPWAY

Kent Archives
Office, Sevenoaks
branch

Window Tax
1712. Sevenoaks
and Riverhead
[U1000/20 02]

Canterbury
Cathedral
Archives and City
Record Office

Hearth Tax, **1670.**
parts of
Canterbury
[BCH/1-3].

LANCASHIRE

Published

Transactions of the Historic Society of Lancashire and Cheshire, vol. **52**, N.S., **16** (for 1900, pubd. 1902), pp. 127-38, has an extract from the *Hearth Tax 1662M* [P.R.O. E.179/250/6] for the **Hd. of West Derby** of all names of those possessing houses with more than three hearths (195); and, from **1673M** [P.R.O. E.179/132/355] of (apparently) all names for Liverpool (252) (probably excluding exempt poor).

Liverpool *Hearth Tax* **1663** [P.R.O. E.179/250/8] in *Liverpool in King Charles II's Time*, by Sir Edward Moore (1667-8), ed. W.F. Irvine, 1899, Appendix, pp. 167-70.

Taxation in Salford Hundred, 1524-1802, by J. Tait, Chetham Soc., N.S., vol. **83**, 1924, pp. 84-119 includes extracts from *Hearth Tax* **1666L** [P.R.O. E.179/250/9] and missing places from **1664L** [E.179/250/11], but note only householders with three or more hearths are abstracted.

Lancashire Association Oath Rolls, 1696, (8,454) ed. W. Gandy, 1921 (republished 1985 by Society of Genealogists). Rolls for part of Lancashire [C.213/138-144]. Index to surnames.

Public Record Office [E.179].

Free and Voluntary Present, 1661-2
County [250/5] (?7,500). Two rolls, one very unwieldy.

Hearth Tax *(Assessments and returns)*
(those available on microfilm from P.R.O. marked §; copies at *Lancashire R.O.* except for E.179/330/3).

1662M. West Derby hd. (part) [250/6 §] (?2,000). Constables' returns, paper, repaired and bound together.
Salford, Blackburn, Leyland hds. [330/3]. Very badly decayed, not repaired, and mostly illegible. includes **Salford hd.**: Withington; **Blackburn hd.**: Pendleton, Rishton; **Leyland hd.**: Whittle le Woods, Charnock Richard. 'Unfit for production'.
(1663). County [250/8 §]. Flattened ms. 1. Salford (6,400); 2. Leyland (2,400); 3. Blackburn (3,200); 4. Lancaster (3,600); 5. Derby (6,800); 6. Lonsdale (1,600). In the Lancs. R.O. catalogue Nos. 4 and 5 are described as Amounderness and West Derby.
1664L. County [250/11 §]. Flattened ms. 1. Lonsdale (5,000); 2. Amounderness (4,000); 3. Blackburn (4,600); 4. Leyland (2,400); 5. Derby (7,000), 1m. missing (Great and Little Crosby, Ince Blundell, Litherland); 6. Salford (9,200); 7. County, hearths walled up (?700).
1665M. County [132/352 §]. Schedule of variations, no names.
(1665). Leyland hd. [132/351 §] (2,000). Annotated. Described by Lancs. R.O. catalogue as Schedule of Variations.

Public Record Office, Hearth Tax continued

1666L. County [250/9 §] (?15,000). Collectors' account, paper returns, VG. Leyland, Amounderness, Lonsdale, Salford, West Derby, Blackburn hds.
1671M. County [250/13 §] (?1,500). Schedule of variations only.
1672M. County [132/356 §] (?450). Schedule of variations only.
1673M. County [132/355 §] (?27,500). Lonsdale, Amounderness, Blackburn, Leyland, West Derby, Salford hds. Liverpool *published*, see above.
(n.d.). County [250/12] (?2,000). Fragments (repaired). Good in parts.

Subsidies
(1663). Blackburn hd. [132/350] (220). Poor legibility on upper half, but OK further down.
Lonsdale hd. [132/348] (165). Ms. sewn head to foot. Some decay at end.
[132/349] (220). Ms. sewn head to foot. Some fading and staining.
[250/7] (?50). Bad condition and legibility.
(n.d.) [250/12, m.10]. Place unknown.

Poll Tax
1660. Blackburn hd. [250/4] (?9,000). Fairly long ms., varying, sewn at top, but quite easy to use. A VG record.
(1667). County [250/10] (300). Certificates of defaulters.
(1677). Leyland hd. [132/358] (?350). Decayed and semi-legible at start, but much better lower down.

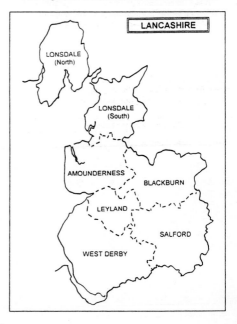

LANCASHIRE

LONSDALE (North)

LONSDALE (South)

AMOUNDERNESS

BLACKBURN

LEYLAND

SALFORD

WEST DERBY

Lancashire: **Public Record Office** continued

Association Oath Rolls, 1695-6 [C.213]
[138] **County;** [139] Duchy Court; [140] **Lancaster;**
[141] **Preston;** [142] **Wigan;** [143] **Clitheroe;**
[144] **Liverpool.**
Part *published.*

Lancashire Record Office, *Preston*

Hearth Tax
Microfilm of all P.R.O. holdings listed except for
E.179/330/3.
1664. Salford, Huncoat and Manchester [QDV
14]. Original returns.
Ainsworth, Birtle, Butterworth, Castleton,
Middleton, Swinton, Thornham, Urmston, Worsley
[UDV 18,19]. Exemptions.
Poll Tax
1678. Bolton division of Salford hd. [QDV 13].

Cumbria Record Office, *Barrow*

Microfilm of Hearth Tax as Lancs R.O., also
Free....Present [E.179/250/5].

Hearth Tax
1679M. Dalton-in-Furness [BD/HJ 174/2].

Manchester Central Library, Local Studies Unit

Hearth Tax
1666L. County. Microfilm of P.R.O. E.179/250/9
[2841].
1666L and 1685(?). Transcript for Oldham,
Chadderton, Royton and Crompton [MF 651].

Subsidies
1663. Billinge (in Wigan) Transcript [LI/10/151/1].

Poll Tax
1690. Manchester [M91/74] (800).
1692. Rochdale (Wuerdle, Wardle and
Blatchinworth townships) [MISC/180].

Wigan Record Office, *Leigh*

Poll Tax: **1694.** Lowton [D/P 17/24/2].

LEICESTERSHIRE

Publications

Hearth Tax, **1666L** [P.R.O. E.179/251/9] in
Leicestershire Medieval Village Notes, G.F.
Farnham, 6 vols. (*c.*1920's), by village (alphabetical
1-4, but more in vols 5-6 see index of places, vol.6)
Some also for 1664L [134/322, sometimes
misprinted as 332], 1664M [251/4], and 1670M
[240/279]. Not complete coverage. Some towns in
vols. 12-17 Leics. Arch. Soc., none for Leicester
itself. Not indexed.
Hearth Tax **1664M** (and L?) [E 179/134/322 and
251/4] in *Leicester and its Inhabitants in 1664, being
a transcript of the Original Hearth Tax Returns etc,*
transcribed and printed by Henry Hartopp,
Leicester, n.d. (typescript index with John Titford,
Yew Tree Farm, Hallfieldgate, Higham, Dbys. DE55
6AG).

Public Record Office [E.179]

Free and Voluntary Present, 1661-2
County [134/317] (3,000). Excellent.

Hearth Tax *(Assessments and returns)*
(those available on microfilm from P.R.O. marked §;
copies of all references are at *Leicestershire R.O.*)

1662M. County [134/322 §] (11,000).
Leicester, East Goscote [375/19 §] (?250).
Fragment, Beeby only place legible. In bad
condition, not repaired.
Sparkenhoe hd. [375/18 §] (?500). In bad
condition, much illegible.
1664M. County [251/4 §] (12,500). Draft. Nine
paper books, by hd., annotated, some exempt
poor shown. VG.
County [251/3 §] (12,500). Enrolment of 251/4.
Broad but quite short ms., easy to use. Annotated,
exempt poor shown.

Leicestershire, P.R.O., Hearth Tax ctd

1665L. County [251/8 §] (?12,000). Draft. Sewn paper sections. Annotated. Exempt poor shown. **County** [251/5 §] (?12,000). Enrolment of 251/8. Bad decay at feet of ms.
1665M. County [251/7 §] (?). Draft. Sewn paper sections. Annotated.
County [251/6 §] (12,200). Enrolment of 251/7. Annotated. Exempt poor not shown.
1666L. County [251/9 §] (10,500). Part *published*. Draft, paper book. Exempt poor not shown.
1670M. County [240/279 §] (15,500).
1673L. County, except Leicester [134/320 §]. 'Views of accounts'. Only alterations since 1672M listed.
(Arrears)
1662M. County [375/12]. Desperate.
1662M-1664L. County with Rutland [371/2]. Partly Latin. Mainly constables' names only. Many ms. faded.

Subsidies
(1663). East Goscote hd. [134/316] (100). Decayed, bad condition and legibility.
1664. Sparkenhoe hd. [134/315] (350).
(1664). Guthlaxton hd. [134/318] (300).

Association Oath Rolls, 1695-6 [C.213] [45] **County.**

| **Leicestershire Record Office**, *Wigston Magna* |

Hearth tax
All P.R.O. Hearth Tax holdings listed are on microfilm at *Leicestershire R.O.* [MF/128-130].

Modern transcripts
County, 1662M and 1664M [P.R.O. E.179/134/322]. Ms, by A.W. Read, indexed by parish name. Also includes **Gartree hd. 1664M** [E.179/251/4].
Loughborough, 1664 [E.179/134/322] (229), TS by A.B. Clarke, 1935. Names arranged alphabetically. Also Knight Thorpe (10) and Woodthorpe (12), 1664.
Loughborough, 1670M [E.179/240/279] (170), alphabetical list of surnames.
Fenny Drayton, 1670 [presumably from E.179/240/279, though incorrect ref. 133/29 is given] (23). TS, with parish register transcript, by W.T. Hall.

Poll Tax
Beaumanor, 1689 [DG9/2806]. Original.

Marriage Tax
Leicester. St. Mary, 1697-99 [BR.IV.2.6] (670);
St. Martin, 1695/6 [BR.IV.2.7];
St. Martin, 1695/6 [BR.IV.2.7] (1,200);
St. Margaret, 1699 [BR.IV.2.8] (840).
Rothley, 1695 [44'28/970/1-9].

LINCOLNSHIRE

Note: Lincoln was assessed separately from the County. The Hearth Tax return for Lincoln in the QS records appears to be the only one to survive.

No published sources, but transcripts at *Lincolnshire Archives Office.*

| **Public Record Office** [E.179] |

Free and Voluntary Present, **1661-2**
County [140/749] (7,500)

Hearth Tax (Assessments and returns)
(1662M). Holland [140/805] (4,000). Some decay, repaired, some loss or illegibility, but mostly OK.
Lindsey [140/806] (3,200). About one third lost from decay, repaired. Most of surviving lists VG legibility and condition, but a few ms. badly faded.
1662M-1664M. County [333] (many). Paper returns, unsorted.
1665M. Holland and **Kesteven** [140/754] (?18,000). In two parts. Annotated.
1670M. Holland and **Kesteven** [140/791] (10,000). Demolished hearths shown.
1671. Lindsey [251/14] (3,500). Schedule of variations.
(Exemption certificates)
1663. County? [334] (many). Unsorted, paper. Marked 'unfit for production' but in fact in good repair.
(Arrears)
1662M-1663M. County [371/3-6, 372/2-5] (450). Latin. Various schedules of sperate, desperate and constables' arrears. Mainly constables' names.

Subsidies

(1663). Holland [140/748] (600).
Lindsey: Lawres, Aslacoe, Corringham, Manley wapentakes [140/750] (500);
Lindsey: same, plus **Well** [140/751] (650).
Kesteven: Langoe wapentake [140/752] (500). Mostly in very bad condition, not repaired.
1665. Lindsey: Louth Eske, Ludborough, Calceworth and **Hill** wapentakes [140/753] (400).
(no date). Lindsey: Gartree wapentake [140/818] (?50). Faded. Very poor legibility.

Poll Tax

1666-67. Assessments: Halton Holgate [140/765] (29); Pinchbeck [140/770] (46). Returns of defaulters [140/756-789; 140/808-817] (mostly less than ten names, but Soxhill 54).
(no date). Lindsey: Candleshoe wapentake [140/804] (1,000).

Association Oath Rolls, **1695-6** [C.213]

[146] **County;** [147] **Lincoln;** [148] **Boston;** [149] **Great Grimsby;** [150] **Stamford;** [151] **Grantham.**

Hearth tax

Original: **Lincoln** city, **1662M**, Lincoln city Quarter Sessions minute book [BROG 1/1, ff.115-124]. Also incl. Waddington, Branston, Canwick and Bracebridge (then incl. in the city's jurisdiction), there may be gaps in its coverage of the city itself. *Transcript:* **Kesteven, 1665M** and **1670M,** TS, based on P.R.O. E.179/140/754, 791. Indexes of places and persons.

Poll Tax (**Candleshoe wap.** except for Hogsthorpe) **1689.** Gunby, Skendleby, Friskney, Bratoft, Partney [Lind. Dep. 35/2/5] (400).
1692. Ashby [Lind. Dep. 35/2/5]; Driby, Friskney, Ingoldmells with Addlethorpe, Orby, Sutterby, Wainfleet [Lind. Dep 35/2/1].
Calcewaith wap. Hogsthorpe [par. 23/4].
1694. Scremby, Winthorpe, Skegness, Steeping Magna, Ingoldmells with Addlethorpe, Orby, Gunby, Firsby, Northolm, Wainfleet, Ashby, Partney, Croft, Irby, and two illegible places [Lind. Dep. 25/2/2] (1,200).
1698. Addlethorpe, Scremby, Candlesby, Irby, Wainfleet, Bratoft, and an illegible place [Lind. Dep. 35/2/5] (500).

Marriage Tax [Lind. Dep. 35/2/7]
~~1***. Sutterby.~~
1701-03. Candleshoe wapentake, incomplete.
1706. Candleshoe wapentake, complete.

LONDON

Publications

London Rate Assessments and Inhabitants' Lists in Guildhall Library and the Corporation of London Records Office, 2nd edn. 1968 (now o.p.), gives details of almost all the relevant lists held in those two repositories - see page 40, after Public Record Office entry.
Guide to the Records at Guildhall, P.E. Jones and R. Smith, 1951 (o.p.), pp. 78-88, 40 XX) in detail.
London Inhabitants within the Walls, 1695, introduction by D.V. Glass, London Record Society, vol. 2, 1966, gives an index to 60,000 names of individuals enumerated in 80 out of 97 parishes within the City walls in connection with the Marriage Tax (see page 7).
'A Supplement to the London Inhabitants List of 1695 compiled by staff at Guildhall Library', *Guildhall Studies in London History,* **2,** 2 and 3 (Apr, Oct 1976), pp.77-104, 136-57. Designed to cover the parishes missing from the Marriage Tax, listed page 40, based on 1694/5 Poll Tax and other sources.

Index (at *Corporation of London R.O.*) to 54,000 individuals in 13 City parishes 'without the walls' not published in the above volume. See under *C.L.R.O.,* page 40.

Public Record Office [E.179]

Free and Voluntary Present, 1661-2
London. Arrears only [252/18] (750). By ward. paper.
Inns of Court. Arrears only [147/608] (11); [252/19] (2).

Hearth Tax (Assessments and returns)
(those available on microfilm from P.R.O. marked §)

1662/3. Tower (Liberty) and **St. Helen (parish)** [252/26 §] (200). Paper book.
(1663). London [252/27 §] (14,000). Slight decay. repaired; opening ms. faded and decayed.
1665M-1666L (+ arrears). **Aldersgate, Bassishaw, Cripplegate Within and Without, St. Andrew Holborn** [147/630] (4,500). Paper book, VG.
(?1665-6). Cornhill, Lime Street, Bishopsgate, Broad Street wards [147/617] (4,000). Paper book, VG.
Farringdon Within and Without wards [147/627] (6,500). Paper book, VG.
1666L. London and Middlesex [252/32] (44,000). 39 paper books, 879ff., annotated. According to CAFM, the following in the City of London are missing: **7.** St. Mary Abchurch, St. Martin Orgars, St. Laurence Orgars, All Hallows the Great and Less; **12.** St. Matthew Friday Street, St. John Evangelist, St. Margaret Moses, St. Nicholas Olave, St. Mary Somerset, St. Mary Mounthaw,

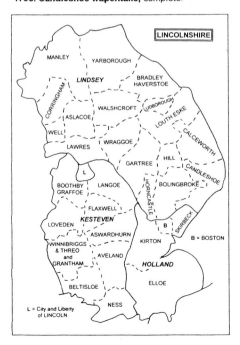

LINCOLNSHIRE

MANLEY

YARBOROUGH

LINDSEY
BRADLEY HAVERSTOE

WALSHCROFT
LUDBOROUGH

ASLACOE
LOUTH ESKE

WELL
WRAGGOE
CALCEWORTH

LAWRES

GARTREE
HILL
CANDLESHOE

BOOTHBY
GRAFFOE
LANGOE
BOLINGBROKE
HORNCASTLE

FLAXWELL
SKIRBECK

KESTEVEN
LOVEDEN
B

ASWARDHURN
WINNIBRIGGS & THREO and GRANTHAM
AVELAND
KIRTON
B = BOSTON

BELTISLOE
HOLLAND
ELLOE

NESS

L = City and Liberty of LINCOLN

London, *Public Record Office, Hearth Tax*, contd.

1666L ctd. St. Nicholas Coleabbey, St. Mary Magdalen Old Fish St. , St. Augustine's; **13.** Ratcliffe, Shadwell; **14.** St. Peter Cornhill, St. Michael Cornhill, St. Martin Outwich, St. Benet Fink, St. Peter le Poore, St. Bartholomew Exchange, St. Margaret Lothbury, St. Stephen Coleman Street, St. Mildred Poultry, St. Mary Woolchurch, St. Christopher, All Hallows by the Wall; **15.** All Hallows Broad Street, St. Mildred's, Holy Trinity the Less, St. Michael Queenhithe, St. James Garlickhill, St. Mary Aldermary, St. Thomas Apostle, St. Martin Vintry; **17.** St. Anne's Blackfriars, St. Andrew by the Wardrobe, St. Benet Paul's Wharf, St. Peter Paul's Wharf; **23** and **24.** St. Botolph's Bishopsgate East.

(pre-1674). London [147/624] (10,000). Ms. sewn at top. Some decay, repaired, fading/staining.

(1674). London [252/23] (?20,000). Much fading. Return of new hearths [252/24] (20). Paper.

1675. New Serjeants Inn [252/25] (16). Paper.

No date. London [252/28] (4,000). Paper book, not repaired, some pages torn and entries lost, some staining.

(arrears)

1664. London [371/7] (700). Desperate.

1670-1. London and Middlesex [252/20] (4,000). Some fading.

(1670-1). London [252/21] (7,000). Latin. 2ms. decayed.

Subsidies

1664. Candlewick Street ward [147/609] (50). Bad condition and legibility.

Tower ward, St. Dunstans in the East [147/610] (200+). Badly faded in parts.

Poll Tax (arrears, certificates of non-payment)

1666-7. Bread Street [147/611] (80); Tower ward [147/613] (80); Lime Street [147/614] (100); Tower of London [147/615] (10).

1678. Farringdon within, Blackfriars [147/612] (75), streets named; [147/618] Includes Coleman Street (28); Vintry (31); Aldersgate without (24); St. Bartholomew the Less (4); Bassetshaw (8); Vintry, Garlickhythe (16); Farringdon without; St. Bride's Middle Precinct (streets named; 150); Cripplegate within, Milk Street (10); Portsoken, High Street (33). [147/619] (300). St. Bride's precinct and Farringdon Without ward. [147/620] (24). St. Sepulchre parish, church precinct. [147/621] (100). St. Martin le Grand. [147/623] (300). St. Bride's precinct.

No date. Portsoken, Houndsditch [252/28a] (160); Holborn Cross [147/622] (25).

Association Oath Rolls, 1695-6 [C.213] [160] Lord Mayor, Aldermen and Common Councilmen; [161-70] Various institutions of the City; [171] Guild Companies (80); [172-75] The Tower of London.

Corporation of London Records Office, PO Box 270, Guildhall, London EC2P 2EJ. (see published Guides, page 39.)

Hearth Tax (Assessments and returns) **c.1670-73 City of London.** A limited number, arranged rather confusingly, partly by ward and partly by parish, but most areas are covered.

Subsidies, Aids, etc. (see Guide, page 39)

1661: some wards.   **1680:** all wards.
1663-4: some wards.   **1683:** most wards.
1666-8: most wards.   **1688-90:** all wards.
1671: some wards.   **1693-4:** all wards.
1673-4: all wards.   **1696-7:** all wards
1677-8: some wards.

Poll Tax
1678, 1689-90, 1692-3: almost all wards.
1694-5, 1698: some wards.

Marriage Tax

1695: All parishes except those listed below. **Index** to persons, parishes 'within the walls' published. London Record Society vol. 2.

Index at CLRO to parishes outside the walls: St. Andrew Holborn (part); St. Bartholomew the Great; the Less; St. Botolph; without Aldersgate: Aldgate (part); and Bishopsgate; St. Bride's; Bridewell precinct; St. Dunstan in the West; St. Giles without Cripplegate; St. Olave Southwark (London Bridge precinct); St. Sepulchre; Whitefriars precinct.

Parishes 'within the walls' for which records do **not** survive, and therefore not indexed in the London R.S. vol. 2, but see Publications (p. 39), *Guildhall Studies in London History:*

Holy Trinity the Less; St. Nicholas: Acons; Cole Abbey; Olave; St. Olave: Hart Street ; Jewry; Silver Street; St. Pancras Soper Lane; St. Peter: le Poer; upon Cornhill; Westcheap; St. Stephen Coleman Street ; Walbrook; St. Swithun London Stone; St. Thomas Apostle; St. Vedas Foster Lane.

British Library (Manuscripts Collection)

Marriage Tax
1696. St. Benet and St. Peter Paul's Wharf [B.M. Adds. Ms 32645, ff.4-11v]

Guildhall Library (Department of Manuscripts)

Marriage Tax
1704. St. Benet Sherehog [MS/7625].

Society of Genealogists and C.L.R.O.

Association Oath Rolls, 1695-6.
City Livery Companies (Apothecaries to Fruiterers only). Corrected proof of unpublished transcript by J.H. Bloom.

MIDDLESEX

Note: Westminster was assessed separately from the County.

Publications
(available in the *Greater London History Library*)

Hearth Tax for **Harrow 1674** [P.R.O. E.179/143/370] (about 300), 'The Harrow Hearth Tax', by G. Glazebrook, in *Middlesex & Hertfordshire Notes and Queries*, vol. **14** (1898), pp.187-90. Indexed

Hearth Tax for **Acton, 1664-1674**, transcribed by A. and T. Harper Smith, in *Acton Past and Present*, **15** (1988).

Hearth Tax for **Staines 1664** [G.L.R.O. MR/TH.6] (218), transcribed by H.A. Randall, in *Staines Local History Society Journal*, **6** (Feb 1972). Indexed.

Hearth Tax for **Ealing, Greenford, Hanwell, Northolt, Perivale, 1664L, 1666L, 1672, 1674L**, also **Ealing** only **1670M**, **?1671, 1672/3**, in *Ealing in the 17th Century*, by K.J. Allison, Ealing Local History Society, Members' Paper No. **4** (1963). [1666L from P.R.O. E.179/252/32; rest from G.L.R.O.]

Poll Tax for **Uxbridge 1693/4**, transcript of assessment for 4s in £, from original *in Corporation of London Record Office*, 6pp. [P.60-33 UXB].

Public Record Office [E.179]

Free and Voluntary Present, 1661-2
Westminster [143/333] (1,600). Enrolled. No occupations. Subscriptions taken at Star Chamber, Lincolns Inn, St. Martin le Grand, Covent Garden, St. Clement's.

Hearth Tax *(Assessments and returns)*

(1662). Ossulstone hd., Tower divn. [253/16] (7,000).
(1662-3). County [253/30] (?5,000). Flattened ms. Badly decayed, not repaired, unusable at present.
1663-4. Elthorne hd. [253/17] Constables' returns: Cowley (11); Harmondsworth (100); Harefield (80); Hillingdon arrears (122); Ickenham (24).
(1664). Ossulstone hd., Holborn divn. [143/336] (many). Very bad decay, feet of many ms. lost, repaired; legibility poor.
Elthorne, Spelthorne and Isleworth hds. [143/405] (2,200). Roll. Considerable decay and fading.
1666L. County (with London). [252/32] (44,000). 39 paper books, 879ff., annotated.
(1674). County [143/370] (38,500). First m. faded.
1675. Westminster [253/25] (9,000). By street. Fading on opening ms.
No date. County [253/29] (6,000). Much decay, repaired. Some loss from fading.
County [143/334] (?4,000). Including one good file of 31ms., other miscellaneous ms. decayed, not repaired.
Bethnal Green [143/390] (54). Bad condition.

Public Record Office, Hearth Tax continued

No date ctd. **Hatton Garden** [143/391] (60).
Tower Hamlets [143/392] (3,000). Flattened ms. Includes 1ms for St. Giles in the Fields.
No date. Westminster [143/404] (1,700). By ward. Repaired but much lost or faded.
Clerkenwell, etc. [143/406] (?3,500). Repaired but badly decayed and faded.
Tower Hamlets [143/407] (20,000). Ms. sewn at head, outer ms. damaged.
? Westminster/Holborn [253/28] (5,000). Some decay, repaired.
(Exemption certificates)
1673-5. County [143/367] (many). Paper certificates from incumbents and churchwardens. VG. Incl. some 1667 *Poll Tax* certificates and arrears.
(Arrears)
1664. Covent Garden, etc. [143/335] (2,500). Paper book.
1665M-1666L. St. Andrew Holborn, St. Giles in the Fields, Saffron Hill [267] (4,000). Paper book, VG.
Gore hd. [268] (1,000). Paper book, VG.
1670-1. County with **London** [252/20] (4,000). Some fading.

Subsidies

1660. Tower Hamlets [143/332] (1,750). VG. Strangers indicated.
1664. Ossulstone hd., Holborn divn. [143/337] (?150). Some decay, not repaired. Much fading but parts O.K.
(1666). Westminster [143/338] (500). Certificates of defaulters.
No date. Westminster [143/385] (?). Badly decayed, some parts legible.
Holborn [143/393] (650). Flattened ms. 2ms. badly decayed, others part decayed but otherwise OK.

41

Middlesex, *Public Record Office* continued

Subsidy or Aid(?)
1671. Tottenham [253/21] (106). By ward.
South Mimms [243/22] (148).
Enfield [243/23] (200).
Edmonton [243/24] (130). By ward (date probably 1671).

Poll Tax (Certificates of defaulters, non payment, arrears).

Note. These certificates are full of evidence of mobility and of considerable interest, worthy of detailed study.

1666. Grays Inn, etc. [143/345] (16).
(1666). Westminster [143/347] (200).
1667. Golden Lane, etc. [143/346] (75).
Holborn [143/353] (250).
Holborn (north) [143/360] (95).
Poplar, Blackwall [143/342] (100).
St. Giles without, Whitecross Street, etc [143/357] (100).
St. James Pall Mall [143/354] (60).
1667. St. Margaret Westminster. Samuel Baker's ward [143/341] (50); Nicholas Uphman's ward [143/355] (113); [238/109] (80) (partly soldiers, absentees).
St. Martin in the Fields [143/349] (200); High Street, upper divn. of [143/352] (55); Edward Ireland's ward [143/358] (100); [253/19] (28); Charing Cross [143/362] (40).
Savoy ward, Duchy of Lancaster [252/33] (100).
Shadwell [143/350] (150).
East Smithfield [143/339] (250).
Spitalfields [143/382] (100). ?1667 ('great loss by late lamentable fire').
Wapping [143/348] (600).
(1677). St. Clement Danes [143/401] (33).
1678. Furnivall's Inn [143/377] (28: actual taxpayers); [147/626] (4).
Grub Street [143/378] (82).
High Holborn [143/381] (300).
Hornsey [143/374] (25).
Limehouse [143/376] (75).
Minories [143/380] (20).
St. Botolph's Bishopsgate without [143/351] (136); [143/379] (250).
St. Clement Danes [143/401] (33).
St. Martin in the Fields [143/371] (100).
Savoy [143/375] (45); [143/386] (35).
Wapping (Ratcliffe Highway) [143/373] (150); (Whitechapel) [143/372] (92).
No date. Bromley [143/399] (15).
Chiswick [143/394] (46).
Clerkenwell [143/398] (82).
Hackney [143/397] (45). Includes Church Street , Mare Street , Well Street, Grove Street.
Hoxton [143/402] (250). **Islington** [143/396] (33).
South Mimms [143/411] (13).
Norton Folgate [143/388] (100).

Middlesex, *Public Record Office, Poll Tax* contd.

1667 ctd. **St. Giles in the Fields:** Old Town divn. [143/387] (25); Old Town divn. with Bloomsbury [143/403] (200); Bloomsbury [143/389] (250).
St. Martin in Fields: Drury lane div. [253/27] (117).
St. Sepulchre Holborn [143/400] (200).
Shoreditch [143/383] (100).
Strand [143/395] (79).
Whitechapel [143/384] (150).

Marriage Tax: Harefield, 1699 [T.64/302]

Association Oath Rolls, **1695-6** [C.213] [152] **County;** [153] Militia officers; [154] Commissioners of tax; (155: Enfield Chase - missing); [156] **Kensington;** [157-58] **Westminster;** [159] **St. Martin le Grand.**

Greater London Record Office, London

Hearth Tax (Assessments and returns)

1664. Enrolled (parchment) copy [MR/TH]: 1. Finsbury divn.; 2. Holborn divn.; 3. Brentford divn.; 4. Tower divn.; 5. Edmonton and Gore hds.; 6. Elthorne, Spelthorne and Isleworth hds.; 7. City and Liberty of Westminster] (43,000). On microfilm except for 5 (Edmonton and Gore hds.) Index to Hornsey, Finchley and Friern Barnet (all Finsbury divn.).
1669-70. 3½ years ending **1670M**, delivered 15 Apr 1672 [MR/TH.8]. Parchment engrossment. Covers most of county except Gore hd., and Westminster.

Note. All the other holdings are original paper returns by constables:
1669 or earlier. **Gore hd.** [MR/TH.75].
1670-71. Ossulstone hd. [MR/TH.9-19; on microfilm M/MIC 26/1-2]. Covers much of hd., environs of London.
Spelthorne hd. [MR/TH.20]. Also typed transcript of Hampton and Hampton Wick at G.L.R.O., open shelves, Catalogue Room, Archive Section.
?1670-71. Edmonton hd. [MR/Th.73-74].
1671-72. St. Giles in the Fields [MR/TH.21].
1672. Edmonton, Elthorne hds. [MR/TH.22,23], paper engrossments. Little Ealing, Old and New Brentford, Gore, Isleworth, parts of Ossulstone hd. [MR.TH.24-38].
1672-73. Ossulstone hd. [MR/TH. 39-42] (Acton, Chiswick, St. Botolph Aldgate, St. Giles in the Fields, Trinity Minories).
1673. Ossulstone hd. [MR/TH.43] (Chelsea, Fulham, Kensington).
1673/4. Ossulstone hd. [MR/TH.44] (St. Giles without Cripplegate, St. Katherine's).
?1674. Ossulstone hd. [MR/TH.45-48]. **Nearly all rest of county, excl. Westminster** [MR/TH.49-72].
No date. Isleworth hd. [MR/TH.76-77].
Ossulstone hd. [MR/TH.78-115].
Spelthorne hd. [MR/TH.166-17].
Note. The G.L.R.O. catalogue lists the places within each hundred with years for which returns survive.

Middlesex continued

Corporation of London Records Office,
PO Box 270, Guildhall, London EC2P 2EJ

See *London Rate Assessments and Inhabitants'*
Lists in the Guildhall Library and C.L.R.O., 2nd
edn., 1968 (out of print).

Assessment for 4s. in the pound (Aid)
1693/4. Most of county (?all).

City of Westminster Archives Centre,
10 St. Ann's Street, London SW1P 2XR

Poll Tax
1664. St. Martin in the Fields. Return of
inhabitants [F4533].

Marriage Tax
1695. St. Margaret's Westminster. Collectors'
books (incomplete) [E1566-69]. St. Margaret's
Long Ditch and Petty France wards, St. Peter
ward, Palace ward.

Society of Genealogists

Hearth Tax, **Isleworth 1664-1674.**

MONMOUTHSHIRE

Public Record Office [E.179]

Free and Voluntary Present, **1661-2**
County [253/32] (3,150). VG. Microfilm or prints
and transcripts with B.Ll. James, South Wales
Record Soc., 8 Grove Ct., Birchgrove, Cardiff
CF4 4QS.

Hearth Tax (Assessments and returns)
(those available on microfilm from P.R.O. marked
§)

1663M(?). County [148/95 §] (4,000). In Latin.
Condition variable. Arrears included. Microfilm
and transcript with South Wales Record Soc.
1664L. County [148/97 §] (3,000). In Latin. Microfilm and transcript with South Wales Record
Soc.
No date. Part of **County** [148/98] (1,800).
Flattened short parchment ms. Decayed at feet
but otherwise generally good legibility. Shows
bakehouses and exempt poor.
Wentloog hd. [253/33] (170). 1m. badly decayed
and mostly illegible; other (120 names) OK.

Monmouthshire, *Public Record Office,* continued

Subsidies
1661. Abergavenny hd. [148/90] (150). By street,
VG.
Usk hd. [148/91] (150). Flattened ms.
1663. Caldicott hd. [148/92] (150). 3ms. sewn head
to foot. Top ms. (Chepstow, Mathern) OK, but
much decay (repaired) and illegibility in remainder
of roll.
Wentlooge hd. [148/93] (70). Flattened ms., two
sewn together. Top OK (Rumney, Michaelstone,
St. Mellons, Bassaleg, Newport), rest decayed.
Ragland hd. [148/94] (50). 2ms. sewn together.
Top ms. OK (Clitha, Bryngwyn, Bettus Newith,
Ragland, Tregare). Remainder decayed, repaired,
but mainly illegible.

Poll Tax
No date. County [148/89] (100). Fragments 2ms.
legible and OK, 2ms. decayed and illegible.
Wentloog hd. [253/34] (1,200). Roll, VG.

Recusants
No date. Caldicott hd. [253/35] (52).

Association Oath Rolls, **1695-6** [C.213].
[176] **County;** [177] Militia Officers;
[178] **Monmouth;** [179] **Newport;** [180] **Usk.**

National Library of Wales, Aberystwyth

Marriage Tax
1699. Bassaleg [Tredegar Mss & Documents,
no. 115].

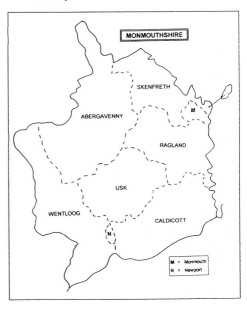

NORFOLK

Note: Norwich was assessed separately from the county.

Publications

An exhaustive account of the surviving *Hearth Tax* records in the Public Record Office has been given by Peter Seaman (himself on the staff of the P.R.O.) in *The Norfolk Ancestor* in 5 parts, vol. **2**, pts. 2, 3, 5, 6, 9 (Sept 1980-June 1982). This makes a detailed description of these records here unnecessary and inappropriate.

Norfolk Hearth Tax Assessment, Michaelmas 1664, transcribed by M.S. Frankel and P.J. Seaman, index by P.T.R. Palgrave-Moore, is published in *Norfolk Genealogy* **15** (1983). The introduction also describes the various HT records in the P.R.O. The **1664M** assessment was dispersed amongst six E.179 references [154/700, 707, 709; 238/119; 253/45; 367/13]. Many of the ms. are in bad condition with poor legibility. Peter Seaman has remarked that 'the original records should only be examined by the serious scholar', and in the case of this meticulous transcript of what is clearly a very difficult source it should be necessary to see these documents only in exceptional circumstances. The assessment (which excludes Norwich) covers about two thirds of the county (18,700) names, the remainder being lost (Blofield, Brothercross hds., most of Great Yarmouth, and parts of other hundreds).

Norfolk and Norwich Hearth Tax Assessment, Lady Day 1666 [E.179/253/42-44], transcribed by P.J. Seaman, is published in *Norfolk Genealogy* **20** (1988). This covers most of Norwich and the hds. of Brothercross, Diss, Earsham, Gallow, Holt, Launditch, North Greenhoe, North Erpingham, Smithdon and Taverham; with partial returns for Clavering, Forehoe and Mitford hds.

'Norwich subscriptions to the voluntary gift of **1662**' [E.179/154/655], transcribed by Miss P.M. Williams, Norfolk Record Society **1** (1931).

See also *Parliamentary Taxation in Seventeenth Century England*, M.J. Braddick, Royal Historical Society Studies in History **70**, 1994. This is based on a detailed study of Norfolk taxation returns.

| Public Record Office [E.179] |

Free and Voluntary Present, 1661-2

County, schedule of collectors' contributions [154/663] (56); **'County'** [253/40] (3,000). Six rolls, mostly short and easy to use, but one very long and unwieldy. Mostly good legibility, but occasional decay and poor legibility.
Includes **Great Yarmouth** (in paper book, VG).
Clavering hd. [154/662] (400); **Diss hd.** [153/618] (300); **North** and **South Erpingham Hds.**, **Eynesford** and **Holt hds.** [154/661] (150); **South Erpingham hd.** [154/664] (200);

Norfolk: *P.R.O., Free & Voluntary Present* contd.

Freebridge Marshland [154/653] (400), some fading; **South Greenhoe hd.** [154/651] (140); **Happing hd.** [154/657] (150); **Henstead hd.** [154/659] (150); **Holt hd.** [154/665] (150) (see also above); **Launditch hd.** [154/660] (300); **Loddon hd.** [154/658] (150); **(Freebridge) Lynn** [253/41] (240); **Norwich** [154/655] (500) (*pubd.*): **Taverham, Blofield, South Walsham hds.** [154/654] (300); **Tunstead hd.** [154/656] (200); **Wayland** and **Grimshoe hds.** [157/12] (200);

Hearth Tax

The documents are described in detail by Peter Seaman in *The Norfolk Ancestor* and in the introduction to the edition of the Norfolk **1664M** assessment.

1662M. Norwich [154/701]. In poor condition.
1664M. County. *Published.*
1666L. County and Norwich [253/42-44]. *Published.*
1672M. County only (not Norwich) [154/697]. Badly damaged by rodents, repaired but much lost.
No date. Clavering and Depwade hds., Barton Bendish in **Clackclose hd.** [154/703a]. In reasonably good condition, one corner eaten away.
Depwade, Diss, Earsham, Eynsford hds. [154/704]. Same assessment and condition as previous references.
(Exemption certificates)
1670-74. County and Norwich [337 and 338]. Paper, many printed.
1671. Smithdon hd. [154/696]. Paper. Sedgford (48) and Stanhow (28) only.
1671-74. County and Norwich [336]. Paper, many printed. Listed by hundred and parish, number of names and date, in *Norfolk Ancestor*, vol. **2**, pts. 6 and 9. Fragile.

Subsidies

1663. South Erpingham hd. [154/666] (150). Some loss from decay, repaired.
North Erpingham, North Greenhoe hds. [154/667] (300).
Eynesford, Holt hds. [154/668] (?500). Bad condition, mostly illegible.
No date. Smithdon hd. [154/710] (150).
Eynesford hd. [153/615] (250).

Poll Tax

1660. Mainly schedules of arrears but may include some assessments. All refs. [E.179/**154**] followed by number shown in square brackets:
[633] Yarmouth (500), variable condition and legibility; [634] Yarmouth (350), end of ms. decayed; [635] S. Greenhoe and Grimshoe hds. (?350); [636] N. & S. Erpingham hds. (25); [637-8] Yarmouth (1,000); [639] Scratby (25); [640] Thrigby (40); [641] Winterton (37); [642] Clippesby (25); [643] Thurne (34);

Norfolk: *Public Record Office, Poll Tax*, contd.

1660 ctd. [644] East Somerton (15), damaged by damp, some names lost; [645] Billockby (18); [647] Yarmouth (400); [648] Herringby (25); [649] Stokesby (50), faded and some names lost from damp; [650] Depwade hd. (425); [706] Diss hd. (?), mostly illegible.
Ref. [E.179/**253**/38] Yarmouth (poor legibility), Askham cum Owby and Runham (200); [253/38a] (320): Sturston, Santon Ho., Bucknam Ho., Sweeting cum Broomhill, Northwold, Methwold, Cranwith, Mundford, Colweston, Igborowe, Standford, Croxton, Merton, Breckles, Watton, Saham Tony, Carbrook, Thompson, Griston, Caston, Threpton, Ellingham cum Rockland, Stowbedon, Tetington, Ashill; [253/38b] Hemsby (90); [276/69b] Martham.
1667. Certificates of defaulters. **Blofield hd.** [154/671] (5).
Ditchingham hd. [154/690] (23).
(1678). County. Certificates of defaulters, etc. [154/698] (?250). Mainly collectors' names but short list of Yarmouth taxpayers.
No date. County. [253/46] (2,500). ?If Poll Tax. Much decay, repaired, legibility variable, but parts OK.

Association Oath Rolls, 1695-6 [C.213]
[181] **County;** [182-84] **Norwich;** [185] **Kings Lynn;** [186] **Yarmouth;** [187] **Thetford.**

Norfolk Record Office, Norwich

Poll Tax
1660. South Erpingham Hd. Separate lists for each parish [Aylsham Collection 202] (4-5,000).
Hearth Tax
North Erpingham Hd.: Hanworth 1662, 1664 [Aylsham Collection 203].

Marriage Tax
Tunstead hd., 1704 [Pet 1047/20/1-26, 266x2] (except Hoveton St. John); North Walsham [Pet.574 99X3] (1,300).
1705 [Pet 1047/21/1-23, 266x2] (except Barton Turf, Beeston St. Lawrence and Sloley).

Norwich city records include:
List of signatories against the Solemn League and Covenant, 1677-1718.
Books of assessments for the 'Royal Ayde', 1664-1725.
Papers relating to hearth tax, 1666-96.
Hearth Tax (incomplete), 1671.
Supply, St. John Maddermarket, 1678.
Royal Aids, 1689 and 1691.
Poll Tax, St. Peter Mancroft and St. Stephen, 1694.
For the King's Navy, St. Saviour, 1699-1700.
Subsidy, St. Clement, 1702.
Land and Window Taxes, 1708-1765.

King's Lynn borough records (on microfilm at *Norfolk Record Office*).

Poll Tax assessments, 1689, 1692, 1694, 1702 [KL/C47/10-25].
Tax assessments, 1702-05.

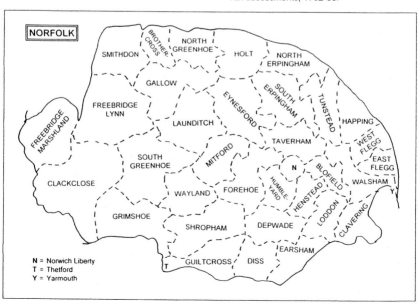

NORTHAMPTONSHIRE

Publication

Hearth Tax for **Grimsbury** and **Nethercote** (N'hants. part of Banbury (Oxon.) parish), **1662M, 1674L** [P.R.O. E.179/254/11,14], included in 'Taxpayers in Restoration Banbury', *Cake and Cockhorse* (Banbury Historical Soc.), vol. **9**, no. 6.

Public Record Office [E.179]

Free and Voluntary Present, 1661-2
County [254/9] (3,000). Enrolled.
Arrears [254/10] (60).

Hearth Tax (Assessments and returns)
(Microfilm copies at *Northamptonshire R.O.*)

1662M. County [254/11] (12,500). Enrolled.
Occasional fading at edges of ms.
Nassaburgh hd. [254/12] (1,750). Enrolled.
(1662M). Northampton [254/15] (500). Paper book.
By ward.
1663M or **1664L. Nassaburgh hd.** [157/450]
(1,000). Ms. sewn end to end, awkward to use.
1670M. County [157/446] (22,000). Good condition and legible, but 'imperfect'.
1674L. County [254/14] (24,000). Enrolled. Some decay at edges.
(Auditor's papers)
1662M-1663M or **1664L. County** [157/468].
A miscellaneous collection of paper books (and one parchment m.), mostly accounts, but including lists of those in arrears at 1663M. Would repay detailed study.
(Arrears)
1662M. County. Sperate [372/2] (50); desperate [372/3] (100), faded: both in Latin.
1663M. County. Sperate [372/4] (60); desperate [372/5] (500). Both in Latin.

Subsidies
(1663). Willybrook, Polebrook, Navisford hds. [254/13] (230).
(1664). Corby, Rothwell, Huxloe, Orlingbury, Higham Ferrers and **Hamfordshoe hds.** [157/448] (1,000).
No date. Corby and **Rothwell hds.** [157/463] (100). Parts badly faded.
Nassaburgh hd. [157/464] (50). 1m. decayed and illegible, 1m. legible.

Poll Tax (?)
1660. Castor [238/130] (100). 1 flat m.
No date. Nassaburgh hd. [157/461] (90). Fragment, 1 flat m., includes Ailsworth, Sutton, Marholm.

Association Oath Rolls, 1695-6 [C.213]
[188] **County;** [189] **Peterborough;** [190] **Northampton;** [191] **Brackley;** [192] **Higham Ferrers.**

Northamptonshire Record Office, Northampton.

All *Hearth Tax* holdings at the P.R.O. are on microfilm at *Northamptonshire. R.O.* [M.25/1,2].

Parliamentary Aid
1691, Rothwell, Corby, Huxloe hds. [M(TM)405-78].

Poll Tax
*c.***1660.** Potterspury [YZ 4397].
1694-5. Rothwell hd. [M(TM)479]; **Corby hd.** [C(TM)89].
1698. Rothwell, Corby hds. [C(TM)91-2]; **Huxloe hd.** [M(TM)480]

Marriage Tax
1697. Rothwell hd. [C(TM)90]. Indexed transcript at *N'hants R.O.* and at the *Society of Genealogists.*

Window Tax
1702. Rothwell, Corby, Huxloe hds. [C(TM)92].

The foregoing tax lists at the N.R.O., all in the Maunsell collection, have mostly been photocopied.

Note. The **1674L** *Hearth Tax* list has (subject to final checking) been transcribed for the Hds. of **Chipping Warden, Corby, Fawsley, Guilsborough, Hamfordshoe, Higham Ferrers, Huxloe, Nobottle Grove, Orlinbury, Polebrook, Rothwell** and **Spelhoe** (this includes Northampton). It is hoped to extend the project to other years also. For details of current access, send s.a.e. (or 2 IRCs) to Mr. Francis Howcutt, 22 Thurlestone Road, West Norwood, London SE27 0PD, who would also be glad to hear from anyone willing to work on areas and years not already covered.

NORTHUMBERLAND

Note. Berwick-on-Tweed, historically in co. Durham but included here under Northumberland, was assessed separately from either county, as was Newcastle-upon-Tyne. The 'North Durham' areas of modern Northumberland - Norhamshire, Islandshire and Bedlingtonshire - are included under Co. Durham.

Publications

Newcastle **1665M** *Hearth Tax* [P.R.O. E.179/ 158/104] (2,510 incl. exempt poor) in 'Newcastle Householders in 1665: Assessment of Hearth Tax', by Richard Welford, *Arch. Aliena,* s. 3, vol. 7, 1911, pp. 49-76.
Northumberland 1664L *Hearth Tax* [from a photocopy 1925 at Northumberland R.O. of P.R.O. E.179/158/103], being published in *Jnl. of Northumberland and Durham FHS,* **8,** 3; **9,** 1,2 (Corbridge), 4 (Hexham); **10,** 1; **20,** 3 (Morpeth) (July 1983 on), transcribed by D.W. Smith. In progress.

Public Record Office [E.179]

Free and Voluntary Present, 1661-2
Berwick-upon-Tweed only [272/37] (174).

Hearth Tax (Assessments and returns)
(those available on microfilm from P.R.O. marked §)

(1662). County [254/17]. Very badly decayed and much illegible.
1664I. County [158/103] (3,500). Photocopy at Northumberland C.R.O. Being *published* in instalments, see above.
 Newcastle [254/20] (1,500). Flat parchment sheets. By ward.
(1664). Newcastle [158/101] (1,750). By ward. Shows exempt poor.
1665 L&M. County [158/106] (5,000). Includes exempt poor.
1665M. Newcastle [158/104] (2,510). *Published.* Enrolled Jan 1666/7.
1666L. County, with Newcastle and Berwick [158/105 §] (14,000). Repaired paper roll, VG.
(1670-71). Newcastle [158/109] (150). Variations/alterations in assessment.
1674L. Berwick-on-Tweed [76/1] (550). VG.
(1674). County [158/110] (10,000).
 Newcastle [254/21] (?1,000). First 2 ms. faded and illegible.
No date. County [254/22] (8,000). 'Unfit for production'. Badly decayed in parts.
 County [254/23]. Badly faded, decayed in part. *(Exemption certificates).*
1667-69. Simonburn, Hartburn [360].
(Arrears)
(1663). County/Newcastle [254/19] (750). By ward.
(1664). County [254/18] (4,000).

Public Record Office continued

Hearth Tax (Arrears) continued
1662-64. Newcastle [372/7,8] (200). Constables' and sperate. Latin. Some fading and poor legibility.
(1665). Newcastle [158/102] (750). Flat parchment ms.
1666L. County [158/99] (1,500). VG.

Subsidy
No date. County [158/113] (750). Sewn head to foot. VG.

Association Oath Rolls, 1695-6 [C.213]
[193] **County;** [194] **Newcastle on Tyne;** [195] **Militia officers;** [196] **Trinity House;** [197] **Morpeth;** [198] **Berwick;** [199] **Alnwick;** [200] **North Shields,** etc.

Northumberland County Record Office, Morpeth Record Centre, Loansdale, Morpeth

Photocopy of *Hearth Tax* **1664** [N.R.O. 1925, of P.R.O. E.179/158/103]. Being published in instalments, see above.

Note. transcripts of Hearth Tax reported to be in the possession of the Society of Antiquaries of Newcastle upon Tyne are in fact only incomplete extracts.

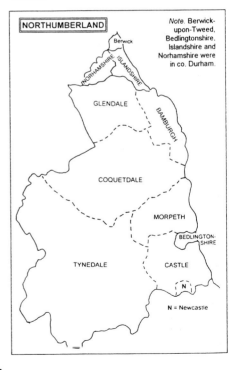

47

NOTTINGHAMSHIRE

Note: Nottingham was assessed separately from the County.

Publications

Hearth Tax, **1664L County,**(dated 15 Jan 1663/4) [P.R.O. E.179/160/320-2, 254/28] (10,473) (except Nottingham town); **1674L County** [E.179/254/30], **Nottingham** [31] (11,888). Exempt poor shown for both years. Indexed. Transcribed by W.F. Webster, Thoroton Society **37** (1988). The 1674L return for Nottingham (only) is also in *Chapters of Nottinghamshire History,* by J. Potter Briscoe (1908) (not indexed).

Subsidy/Aid, **1689** [Notts. R.O. DD MH 1/1-97]. First published as *Nottinghamshire Subsidies 1689,* ed. George Marshall, 1895. Re-edited by W.F. Webster and published by Notts FHS, records series vol. **24**, pts. 1 and 2, 1983 (now out of print). Indexed. Part of county only.

Aid, **1689-90,** [P.R.O. E.179/254/34a] (1,000). **Broxtowe hd.** (39 places). Notts FHS vol. **50,** transcribed by W.F. Webster

Association Oath Rolls 1695-6 [P.R.O. C.213/201-204]. For county (nobility, gentry, clerics) and Nottingham, East Retford and Newark (general inhabitants). Notts FHS vol. **50,** transcribed by W.F. Webster.

Public Record Office [E.179]

Hearth Tax (Assessments and returns) (those available on microfilm from P.R.O. marked §; documents for 1663, 1664 and 1674, as published, are at the *Nottinghamshire Record Office.*)

1662M. County except North Clay division of Bassetlaw [254/27 §] (?5,000). Flattened parchment ms. bound in 6 parts, each with contents lists by CAFM. Considerable decay, repaired, and some fading at feet of ms. Otherwise adequate legibility.

(?1662). Bingham hd. [160/329 §] (400). Eleven places only.

Thurgarton hd. [160/330 §] (1,300). Most of hd. (54 places).

Newark hd. [254/33 §] (1,250). Badly decayed, but many names legible.

Bingham and **Rushcliffe hds.** [254/34 §] (1,000). A duplicate of parts of 160/329 and 160/331. Small parts eaten away, but mainly legible.

1664L. County (except Nottingham). **Hds.** of **Bassetlaw** [160/322 §]; **Broxtowe, Rushcliffe** and **Bingham** [254/28 §]; **Thurgarton** and **Newark,** and **Newark** town [160/320 §]. *Published,* see above.

(1670). Bassetlaw and Broxtowe hds. [254/29 §] (1,800). Incl. North Clay div. (5 places), Broxtowe hd. (17 places?) and Bassetlaw hd. (Hatfield div., 17 places?, South Clay div. 29 places). Decayed in parts, repaired.

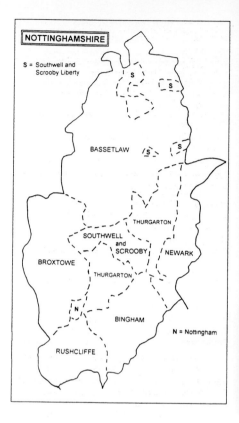

NOTTINGHAMSHIRE

S = Southwell and Scrooby Liberty

BASSETLAW

THURGARTON

SOUTHWELL and SCROOBY

NEWARK

BROXTOWE

THURGARTON

BINGHAM

N = Nottingham

RUSHCLIFFE

Public Record Office, Hearth Tax, continued

1674L. County [254/30 §] (10,919). *Published.* **Nottingham** [254/31 §] (969). *Published.* *(Arrears)*

1663. Nottingham and **County** [160/321] (250). Sperate arrears.

Subsidies

(1664). Bassetlaw hd. [160/323] (500). Decayed and/or faded in parts.

No date. Bassetlaw hd. [160/324] (100). 1ms. reasonable OK, remainder decayed and illegible.

Aid

1689-90. Broxtowe hd. [254/34a] (1,000). *Published.*

Association Oath Roll, **1695-6** [C.213] [201-204]. *Published.*

Hearth Tax
?1661. Bassetlaw hd. [DD.3P 18/1]. North Clay, South Clay and Hatfield divisions. This is definitely dated '1661' and also described as 'Hearth Money', though the Tax was not introduced until 1662.
1670 Arnold [DD 241/11]. Typescript copy of P.R.O. E.179/254/29 (70).
1663-4, 1674. Microfilm of published P.R.O. records.

Subsidies
1663. Bassetlaw hd., Newark hd. (part) [DD.N 230]
1671, 1673. Eakring [DD.SR 216/9-10].

Subsidy/Aid/Land Tax
1689. County (part only) [DD MH 1/1-97]. *Published*, see left.

Marriage Tax
1696. Hucknall Torkard [PR 5363 and 5363e].

Land Tax
1697-1707. West Bridgford [DD.PF 123107-108].

OXFORDSHIRE

Publications

Hearth Tax for **County, 1665M** [P.R.O. E.179/ 164/513] (9,000) in *Hearth Tax Returns, Oxfordshire*, 1665, ed. Maureen M.B. Weinstock Oxfordshire Record Soc. vol. **21**, 1940. The introduction discusses alternative records for 1662 and 1665. **Appx. A:** totals only, comparison of 1665M and 1662M [E.179/255/4] for Ploughley, Lewknor, Binfield, Bloxham, Wootton and Bampton hds.; **Appx. B:** transcript of *Subsidy* return for **Bullingdon hd., 1663** [E.179/164/503] (400); **Appx. G:** *Poll Tax* return for **Taynton, 1666** (160) [original lost]; *Hearth Tax* **1662M** for **Taynton** [E.179/255/4] (34). Index of places only.
Index of personal names to above book, *Index to Oxfordshire Hearth Tax Returns, Michaelmas 1665*, compiled by Jeremy Geere, Oxfordshire FHS, 1985.
Hearth Tax for **Oxford** city, **1665L** [P.R.O. E.179/164/514] (998) in *Surveys and Tokens*, ed. H.E. Salter, Oxford Historical Soc., vol. **75**, 1923, pp. 183-212. Salter suggests this is for 1665**M** for no reason except that the 1662 return [255/4] was for Michaelmas. As 164/513 is specifically dated 1665**M**, it seems likely that 164/514 is for 1665**L**. This return was first published in Oxford Historical Soc., vol. **18**, 1890-1, pp. 75-95, ed. T. Rogers (indexed), but the later edition contains corrections and is more logically arranged.
Vol. **75** also includes an *Aid* for **1667** [Oxford City Archives, p. 5.8] (1,600), pp. 337-54, and a *Poll Tax* for **1666/7** [City Archives, P.5.7.] (8,566), pp. 213-336. Indexed. Not including St. Clements.

Oxfordshire, Publications continued

Banbury (including Neithrop and Grimsbury): 'Taxpayers in Restoration Banbury', by J.S.W. Gibson, *Cake and Cockhorse* (Banbury Historical Soc.), **9**, 6 (Summer 1984), lists alphabetically all names (292) appearing in the *Free and Voluntary Present* **1661** [P.R.O. E.179/255/5], the *Hearth Tax* of **1662M**, Constables' returns [E.179/255/4; Grimsbury, Nhants, enrolled return, E.179/254/11], **1665L&M** [E.179/164/514,513] and **1674L** [Grimsbury, Nhants, only E.179/254/14] and *Subsidy* for **1663** [E.179/164/507]. Hearths, sums paid, spellings etc. compared.
Caversham - see Berkshire, with Reading.
Association Oath Roll. Banbury (*C&CH* **10**,4); Woodstock (*Oxon FH* **4**,2).
Dean, Lidstone, Chalford, Broadstone (Enstone and Spelsbury parishes) in *Hearth Tax* **1662M** [E.179/255/3].

Public Record Office [E.179]

(those available on microfilm from P.R.O. marked §)

Free and Voluntary Present, 1661-2
County [255/5 §] (many). Most (?all) of county in large and unwieldy roll. Several separate ms. (?duplicates, arrears) and one paper book (**Ewelme hd.**). The roll for **Oxford** appears to be signed by at least some of the contributors. Transcription in progress from photocopy for eventual publication. **Banbury** *published*.

Hearth Tax (Assessments and returns)
1662M. County [255/4 §] (?10,000). Constables' paper returns, repaired and bound together, in three books. Arranged by hd.; VG and easy to use. They give far more names and greater accuracy than the 1665 enrolled returns. With next have been transcribed for publication.
County [255/3] (many). Constables' paper returns. Loose sheets, repaired. No special order. Not clear if these are duplicates or additional to 255/4.
Henley-on-Thames [255/6]. Paper book, repaired, VG. Not clear if duplicate of or additional to 255/4.
County [164/504]. Enrolled copy. Badly decayed (eaten by rodents), legibility difficult. Better to use 255/4.
Note. The whole of the 1662M Hearth Tax has been transcribed and indexed by Gwyn de Jong, and is to be published in due course. Meanwhile a photocopy of the enrolled copy [E.179/164/504] is available at *Oxfordshire Archives*.
1665L. County [164/514] (8,000). Early ms. faded and in bad condition. Oxford city and Banbury *published*.
1665M. County [164/513] (9,000). Includes exempt poor. *Published*.
(Arrears)
1663M. County [372/10] (75). Sperate.
1664L. Bullingdon, Ewelme, Bloxham hds. [164/506] (75). Mainly constables' names.

Oxfordshire continued

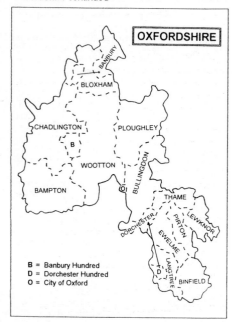

OXFORDSHIRE

B = Banbury Hundred
D = Dorchester Hundred
O = City of Oxford

Public Record Office, continued

Subsidies
1663. Bullingdon, Thame, Dorchester hds.
[164/503] (1,000). Parchment book. Bullingdon
hd. *published.*
Banbury and **Bloxham hds.** [164/507] (300).
Banbury parish *published.*
1664/5. Banbury and **Bloxham hds.** [164/509]
(150). Flat parchment sheet. In four columns, first
column (incl. Banbury town) decayed (repaired)
and illegible, remainder OK.

Association Oath Rolls, **1695-6** [C.213]
[205-06] **County**; [207] **Postcomb**; [208] **Oxford**;
[209] **Woodstock** (*published, Oxon FH*);
[210] **Banbury** (*published, C&CH*).

Bodleian Library, Oxford

Hearth Tax. **1662M. County** [Microfilm MS Film
182, of P.R.O. E.179/255/4]. A photocopy of this
is at *Oxfordshire Archives.*

| *Oxford City Archives,* c/o Centre for Oxfordshire
Studies, Oxford Central Library, Westgate, Oxford.
(48 hours notice required) |
| --- |

Various taxes, etc. (City and Binsey; not
St. Clement's parish).
1667. *Poll Tax* [P.5.7] (8,566). *Published,* Oxford
Historical Soc., **75**.

Oxford City Archives continued

1667-68. *Aid* [P.5.8] (1,500). Six assessments
between Sep 1667 and Dec 1668. One *published*
in Oxford Historical Soc. **75**.
1692-94. *Poll Tax* [P.5.9] (1,500). Six assessments
for the three years, and appeals.
1694. *Poll Tax* [P.5.10] (1,500); **1695/6** appeals
only. **1696** *Aid* (2,000). **1696.** Window Tax
(1,500). Subsequent years give parish totals and
collectors' names only.
1695. *Marriage Tax* (5 parishes only) [P.5.10, back
end of book] (210). Actual names, by parish. Total
sums only for each parish, 1697, 1699,
1700,1702, 1703, 1704, 1705.
1702. *Poll Tax* [F.4.6] (3,250). Book gives names by
parishes (as do all the above) followed by column
for value of stock in trade, money at interest,
pensions and annuities, offices @ 1s. in £,
professions, practices and employments (sums of
money only), 4s. per head, yearly rents and
offices, sum to be charged.

RUTLAND

Publication

Hearth Tax, **1665M** [P.R.O. E.179/255/10], ed. Jill
Bourne and Amanda Goode, Rutland Record
Society, 1991. Indexed.

Public Record Office [E.179]

Free and Voluntary Present, **1661-2**
County [255/7] (1,500). Ms. sewn head to foot.

RUTLAND

Rutland, *Public Record Office,* continued

Hearth Tax (Assessments and returns)
(those available on microfilm from P.R.O. marked §;
copies and transcripts of all references are at the
Leicestershire Record Office.)

1664M. County [255/9 §] (3,200). Flattened
parchment sheets, annotated.
1665L. County [255/11 §]. As 255/10. Includes
non-chargeable.
1665M. County [255/10 §] (?3,500). Exempt poor
included. *Published.*
(Arrears)
See Leicestershire, page 38.

Subsidies
(1663). County [165/195] (300). Badly decayed but
repaired and usable.
East hd. [255/8]. Too fragile to examine.

Association Oath Roll, **1695-6** [C.213]
[211] **Rutland.**

Leicestershire Record Office, Wigston Magna

Hearth Tax
All P.R.O. *Hearth Tax* holdings listed above are on
microfilm at *Leicestershire Record Office*
[MF/130].
Transcript: **County, 1664M** [from P.R.O. E.179/
255/9]. TS, by A.B. Clarke, 1948, names index by
C.V. Appleton, 1949. Hds. of Alstoe, East,
Oakham Soke, Martingley and Wrangdike.

SHROPSHIRE

Publications

Hearth Tax, **1672M, County** [P.R.O. E.179/
168/216] (16,380, originally 17,737), in the
*Shropshire Hearth-Tax Roll of 1672: being a list of
the Householders in the County,* transcribed by
Miss L. Drucker with an introduction by W. Watkins-
Pitchford, Shropshire Arch. and Parish Register
Soc., 1949. Paupers not identified. Fully indexed.
List of 60 places missing from roll.
Poll Tax for **Ludlow, 1667** [P.R.O E.170/255/37]
(1,300), in 'The Ludlow Poll Tax Return of 1667',
Shropshire Arch. Soc. *Transactions,* No. **59**, 1972,
pp. 104-123. Includes two HT exemption certificates
[presumably from E.179/342]. Not indexed.
'The Late 17th Century Tax Lists of the Borough
of Shrewsbury and its Liberties', by Janice
Capewell, *Shropshire FHS Journal,* **5,** 2 (June
1984).

Shropshire continued

Public Record Office [E.179]

Free and Voluntary Present, **1661-2**
County [168/214] (7,500). Not obviously arranged
by place, so probably difficult to use.

Hearth Tax (Assessments and returns).
(those available on microfilm from P.R.O. marked §)

1662M. County [255/35 §] (8,500). Decay at feet of
ms., repaired. Much fading but most adequately
legible. Introduction and contents lists by CAFM.
Brimstree hd. [255/23] (?750). Paper returns by
constables, separate sheets, in roll. Slight decay
in places.
Albrighton [358] (50). Constable's paper return
(stray).
1663M. County [255/24] (many). Paper returns in
bundles in no obvious order; including list of
exempt poor and schedule of arrears.
1672M. County [168/216] (16,380, originally
17,737). 1m. lost, feet of many ms. mutilated.
Published, see left.
?1662-1674. ?County [342] (many). A box full of a
great many paper rolls, constables' returns,
exemption certificates, etc., 1662-1670s. No
attempt made at detailed examination.
(Arrears)
1662-1664. County [255/33,34; 373/1-7] (900).

Subsidies
(1663). Oswestry hd. [255/25] (21).
(1664). North Bradford hd. [255/26] (200).
Ford hd. [255/27] (80).
Ludlow [255/28] (28).
Oswestry hd. [255/29] (120).
Pimhill hd. [255/30] (130).
Shrewsbury [255/31] (250).
Stottesden and **Brimstree hds.** [255/32] (250).
(1666). North Bradford hd. [168/215] (196). Dated
18 CII on cover, but ?1671 inside.

Poll Tax
(1660). Wenlock [168/219] (2,500).
South Bradford hd. [168/220] (5,000).
North Bradford hd. [255/21] (5,000).
Chirbury, Purslow and Clun hds. [255/22]
(5,000).
(1667). Ludlow [255/37] (500). *Published,* see left.
The foregoing poll tax lists indicate wives, give
servants' names, etc.
1678. County [168/217] (300). Poll Tax or Aid ?
Mainly collectors' names only, but some lists of
?defaulters, including some for Shrewsbury.

Association Oath Rolls, **1695-6** [C.213]
[212] County; [213] Militia Officers;
[214] **Shrewsbury;** [215] **Bridgnorth;**
[216] **Ludlow;** [217] **Wenlock;**
[218] **Bishops Castle;** [219] **Oswestry.**

Shropshire continued

Shrewsbury Borough Records (see 'The Late 17th Century Tax Lists of the Borough of Shrewsbury and its Liberties', Janice Capewell, SFHS *Journal*, 5.2). This is a particularly good collection of tax lists. All the bundles cover the town and the 'Liberties' (some 45 places, the equivalent of a hundred) unless otherwise stated. Most are Aids or Subsidies of some sort; other taxes indicated. All references should be preceded by '3365'.
*** = a large, full bundle of lists;
** = a middling size bundle of lists;
* = a small bundle of lists.

239-40. **1660.** Poll Tax ***.
241-42. **1661.** *.
243. **1662.** Some Liberties only *.
244. **1663.** *.
245. **1663.** Town only *.
246. **1664/5.** ***.
247-51. **1665-7.** **.
253. **1672-7.** ***.
254. **1673.** *.
255. **1678.** Poll Tax ***.
256. **1679.** *.
257. *c.1680.* One list for town only *.

Shrewsbury Borough records continued

258. **1689.** Poll Tax ***.
259. **1689.** Trophies money, Town only *.
260-61. **1690-2.** ***.
263. **1694.** Poll Tax ***.
264. **No date.** One list for part of Liberties only (incomplete) *.
266. **1697.** Castle ward in town only *.
267. **1698.** Poll Tax ***.
268. **1702.** Poll Tax/Land Tax ***.
269. **1702.** Poll Tax. Stone Ward in town only *.
272. temp. Anne? Collector's book, Castle Ward in town only *.

Marriage Tax
275-79. **1695-1702.** *Full* censuses of the whole population ***. *Shropshire Records and Research* has a transcript of the tax lists for the town.

Land Tax
280. early C18.*.

House and Window Tax
289. **1698-9.** ***.
290. **1710.** Abbey Foregate only *.
291. *c.1715.* Welsh and Castle Wards *.

Bridgnorth
Poll Tax: **1689.** [SRO 4001/f/8/164]***.

Ludlow
Poll Tax: **1689** [LB8/3/42-43];
1692 [LB8/3/47],
1693 [LB8/3/49],
1698 [LB8/3/53].
Window Tax: **1696, 1699, 1704-08** [LB8/3/85-91]. Covers part of Ludlow only except for 1705.
Land Tax: **1699, 1700, 1702-08** [LB8/156-164]. 1699 and 1702 covers all Ludlow, rest part only.

Munslow hd., co. Salop., subsidy book. 1641-1664 [D(W)1788 p.46 B.8].
Church Stretton, co.Salop., Poll Tax. 1666/7.
[D(W) 1788 p.46 B.8].

B = BRIDGNORTH

SOMERSET

(for **Bristol** see under Gloucestershire)

Publications

Free and Voluntary Present **1661-2, Williton and Freemanors**, and **Carhampton hds**. [P.R.O. E.179/ 256/10] (750), in 'A Benevolence granted to Charles II by the Hundreds of Williton and Freemanors and Carhampton', by Emanuel Green, Somerset Arch. Soc., **35**, 1889, pp.52-83. Not indexed.

Hearth Tax, **1665M**, for **County** [P.R.O. E.179/ 256/16] (5,400). Published in *Hearth Tax for Somerset, 1664-5,* transcribed by R. Holworthy, *Dwelly's National Records,* vol. **1**, 1916. Annotated. Indexed. [Also includes E.179/172/440, 172/485, 256/18-20, 270/36].

Subsidy, **1663**, for **Abdick, Crewkerne, Kingsbury East** and **South Petherton** [P.R.O. E.179/256/17] (800) and certificates of exemption (?) [E.179/172/441] (200), published in *Dwelly's National Records,* vol. **2**, *Directory of Somerset,* transcribed by E. Dwelly, 1929, pt.1, pp. 1-32.

Hearth Tax, Exemption certificates, **1670** [P.R.O. E.179/172/434 and Bundle 343] *Dwelly's National Records,* vol. **2**, pt. 1 (1929), pp. 32-64, **Abdick and Bulstone** to **Catsash hds.** (3,250); pt. **2** (1929), pp. 65-128, **Chew Magna** to **North Curry hds.** (6,400); pt.3 (1931), pp.129-192, **North Curry** to **Williton and Freemanors hds.** (6,400); pt.4 (1932), pp.193-211, **Williton and Freemanors** to **Winterstoke hds.** (1,850).

Publications continued

Hearth Tax, Exemption certificates, **1673-74** [all Bundle 343], pp. 211-56, **Abdick and Bulstone** to **Frome hds.** (4,500); pt. **5** (1932), pp. 257-320, **Frome** to **Wellow hds.** (Wynterton parish) (6,400); not completed, but see below.

Dwelly's Index to the Somerset Hearth Tax Exemption Certificates of 1670 and 1674 with a Completion of Part 5 of Dwelly's National Records vol. 2 (115pp.), published by T.L.Stoate, 1976. This completes vol. 2 with an index to the whole volume, from the original at the *Society of Genealogists.*

| **Public Record Office** [E.179] |

Free and Voluntary Present, **1661-2** (transcript at *Somerset Record Office*)

Houndsborough, Tintinhull, Martock, Somerton and **Stone hds.** [172/424] (1,000). Paper book. VG.

Wells Forum, Glaston and **Whitston hds.** [256/9] (1,000). Paper book,.

Williton and Freemanors, and **Carhampton hds.** [256/10] (750). Paper book. Published in Somerset Arch. Soc., vol. **35**.

Bruton, Catsash, Norton Ferris and **Horethorn hds.** [256/11] (1,100). Paper book.

Whitley, Huntspill, North Petherton, Andersfield and **Cannington hds.** [256/12] (1,250). Paper book.

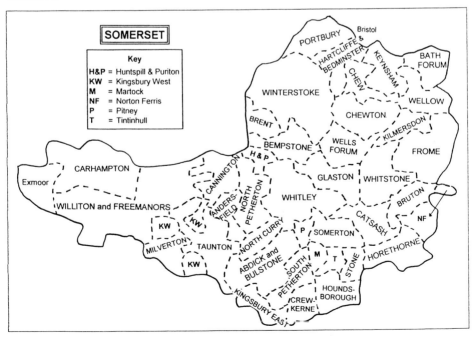

53

Somerset: *Public Record Office, Free and Voluntary Present, 1661-2,* continued

Bridgwater [256/13] (200). Paper book.
Frome, Kilmersdon, Wellow and **Bath Forum** [256/15] (350). Paper book.
Chew, Chewton and **Keynsham hds.** [256/14] (400). Paper book. Transcript by Dwelly at *Society of Genealogists.*

Hearth Tax (Assessment and returns)
(those available on microfilm from P.R.O. marked §)

1665M. County [256/16 §]. Twelve hundreds only, in 18 books. *Published.* Based on 1662M return.
No date. 'County' [256/20] (150). In bad condition but legible: for Dinington, West Bradley, Charleton, Rill als Pill. Published in *Dwelly*, vol. **1.**
Keynsham hd. [172/440] (200). Flat ms. *Published* in *Dwelly*, vol. **1.**
(Exemption certificates)
1670. County (except Bath Forum) [343] (very many). Printed paper forms. *Published.*
1674. County [172/434] (many). Printed paper forms. *Published.*
(Arrears)
1662M. County [373/8,9]. Constables' and sperate. Latin.

Subsidies
1663. Abdick, Crewkerne, Kingsbury East and **South Petherton hds.** [256/17] (?500). *Published.*
(1663). Andersfield, Cannington, Huntspill and **Puriton, North Petherton** and **Whitley hds.** [172/422] (2,750).
(1663-4). Houndsborough, Tintinhull, Stone, Somerton, Martock, Coker(?) and **Pitney hds.** [172/423] (800); [172/426] (1,500). Slight decay, repaired.
No date. Frome, Kilmersdon, Bath Forum and **Wellow hds.** [172/439] (400). Some decay and fading, but mostly OK.

Poll Tax
1660. Portbury, Bempstone, and **Hartcliffe and Bedminster hds.** [172/416] (2,500). Some ms. badly faded, but much OK.
Brent [172/417] (150). Some decay, considerable fading, but parts OK.
North Curry, Milverton, Taunton and **West Kingsbury hds.** [172/418] (2,000). Mainly OK, but some ms. badly faded and occasional decay.
Winterstoke hd. [256/7] (900). Stained and faded, poor legibility.
Bath [256/8] (900). Paper book.

Association Oath Rolls, **1695-6** [C.213]
[220] **County;** [221] Militia officers;
[222] Nonconformists; [225] **Bath;** [226] **Taunton;**
[227] **Bridgwater;** [228] **Minehead;** [229] **Ilchester;**
[230] **Milburn Port;** [231] **Crewkerne;** [232] **Bruton;**
[233] **Langport;** [234] **Axbridge;** [235] **Wellington;**
[236] **Chard;** [237] **Yeovil;** [238] **Ilminster;**
[239] **Frome Selwood.**

Somerset Record Office, *Taunton*

Free and Voluntary Present, **1661-2**
Transcript of 23 hundreds - probably all those listed at P.R.O.

Subsidies
Williton and Freemanors hd., 1665
[DD/WY Box 34]

Aids etc.
Street and Leigh tithing, 1662 [DD/TOR 262].
Stogumber parish, 1664 [DD/WY Bx 29].
Ruishton parish, 1673 [DD/SP 450].
Andersfield hd., 1696 [DD/DP 24/5a].
Wells, 1703 [DD/SAS PR 163]

Poll Tax
Williton and Freemanors hd., 1666
[DD/WY Box 34].
Wells (3 streets only) 1702 [DD/WM 1/410].

Window Tax
Ashill, 1700 [D/P/ashl 23/3].

Land Tax
Bawdrip,
Crandon tithings, 1693-96 [DD/CH Bx 47]
Biddisham, 1711 [D/P/bid. 2/1/1].
Carhampton from 1709 [DD/L 42/16].
Dunster, 1710 [DD/L 33/47].
Glastonbury, 1704 [DD/DN 176].
Lympsham, 1689, 1715 [DD/DN 185].
Minehead, 1710 [DD/L 1/51/26].
Wyndham estates, 1712-16 [DD/WY Bx 161].
Wells borough, from 1679 [DD/FS 72].

Marriage Tax
Wembdon, 1696, 1698 [D/P/wem 23/1].
Langford Budville, 1704 [DD/SF 1869].

STAFFORDSHIRE

Note: Lichfield was assessed separately from the County.

Publications

Hearth Tax, **1665M,** for **County** [P.R.O. E.179/ 256/31], in Staffordshire Record Society *Collections for a History of Staffordshire,* William Salt Arch.Soc. **Pirehill hd.,** 1921, pp. 41-173 (6,500). **Seisdon and Offlow hds.** (excl. Lichfield), 1923, pp. 47-258 (10,500). **Totmanslow hd.,** 1925, pp.155-252 (4,250). **Cuttlestone hd.,** 1927, .pp.1-79 (3,700). Names for **Rugeley** and **Brereton** alphabetically arranged and annotated. All transcribed by E. Grogan. Published version entitled '1666', because finally dated 1 June 1666, and delivered between 9 Jan 1665/6 and 2 Apr 1666, but collected for 1665M. Exempt poor shown. Index to places but not personal names.
Hearth Tax, **Lichfield, no date** [P.R.O. E.179/ 256/35] (380), annotated, and **1662M,** exempt poor and arrears [E.179/324] (200), S.R.S., *Collections,* William Salt Archa\eological Society, 1936, pp.143-77, transcribed by P. Laithwaite. Index to places but not to personal names.
Hearth Tax, **1665, Bushbury,** in *Bushbury Parish and People,* A.H. Chatwin, 1983. Not indexed.

Public Record Office [E.179]

Note. The class number for these documents is E.179; thus for the first below, it should read in full: E.179/179/329. All references must be preceded by E.179.

Free and Voluntary Present, 1661-2

County, including **Lichfield** [179/329] (7,750). Lichfield by street.

Hearth Tax *(Assessments and returns)*
(those available on microfilm from P.R.O. marked §)

1662M. Totmonslow hd. [179/331] (3,500). Some decay and fading.
Pirehill hd. [179/332] (3,500). Introduction by CAFM. Stafford, Hopton, Hilderson and Hulton wanting. Considerable decay, repaired, and fading, but much OK.
1664L. Lichfield [375/2] (?250). Badly decayed, repaired, and faded; very little legible.
1665M. County (excl. Lichfield) [256/31 §] (25,000). *Published.*
1671M. County [256/33] (?500). Variations of assessment. Badly decayed, not repaired.
1672M. County (excl.Lichfield) [256/32]
1.**Pirehill hd.** (4,000). Roll. Considerable decay, not repaired. Some fading and poor legibility, but much OK.
2.**Cuttlestone hd.** (1,500). Flat, some decay, as 1.
3.**Seisdon hd.** (1,750). Roll. Some decay, legibility OK.

Public Record Office, Hearth Tax, 1672M contd.

4.**Totmonslow hd.** (2,750). Flat. Decay repaired, variable legibility. Contents list by CAFM.
5.**Offlow hd.** Virtually all missing.
1673M. County [179/329] (15,000).
No date. Lichfield [256/35]. Paper book. *Published.* **Lichfield,** The Close [256/36] (33). Book.
(Arrears and Exemption certificates)
1662 (Nov). Lichfield [179/324] (200). Paper list of exempt poor, by street. Also arrears. *Published.*
1662M (dated 1664). **Stafford,** and **Pirehill** and **Offlow hds.** [179/334] (250). Certificates of poverty, paper. Some decay.
(1663). County [256/28] (150). Arrears.
1663M-1664L. County [373/10-12]. Arrears.

Subsidies
(1662). Stafford and Pirehill hd. [179/330a] (250). Some decay and fading.
(1663). Offlow hd. [179/323] (200).
No date. Pirehill hd. [179/171a] (42).

Poll Tax
(1660). Cuttlestone hd. [256/27] (350). Paper book.
(1671). Offlow hd. [256/26] (3,300). VG.

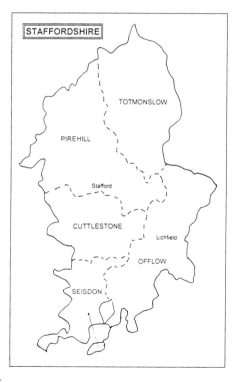

STAFFORDSHIRE

TOTMONSLOW

PIREHILL

Stafford

CUTTLESTONE

Lichfield

OFFLOW

SEISDON

Association Oath Rolls, 1695-6 [C.213]
[257] **Pirehill** etc: [258] **Seisdon** etc;
[259] **County**, Deputy Lieutenants etc;
[260] **Stafford**; [261] **Newcastle under Lyme**;
[262] **Tamworth**; [263] **Uttoxeter and Lichfield.**

Staffordshire Record Office, Stafford

Poll Tax
Cuttlestone hd., 1666 [D260/M/E/429/19].
Ranton Abbey, 1678 [D615/E(X)/4].

Marriage Tax
Bilston, **1695** [D667/3/1].

Window Tax
Cuttlestone hd., 1711 [D260/M/E/429/19].

British Library Manuscripts Collection

Marriage Tax(?)
Lichfield, *c.*1695 [Harleian Mss. 7022]. Ages given.
See 'Lichfield Population List', Francis Howcutt
and Sir Mervyn Medlycott, *Genealogists'*
Magazine, **23**, 9 (March 1991), p. 340.

Warwickshire Record Office, Warwick

Land Tax
1692-3. Rugeley, Brereton and Cannock Wood
[Landor papers CR931/194].

Shakespeare's Birthplace R.O., Stratford

1690. Hamstall Ridware [DR.18/22/6].

SUFFOLK

Publications

Hearth Tax, **1674L,** for **County** [P.R.O. E.179/
257/14] (28,400), in *Suffolk in 1674,* ed. S.H.A.
Hervey, Suffolk Green Books, No. 11, vol. **13**, 1905.
Exempt poor sometimes shown. Indexed.
'The Hearth Tax Returns for the Hundred of
Blackbourne, 1662M' [Suffolk R.O., HD.1538]
(1,070), trans. S. Colman, *Proc. of the Suffolk Inst.*
of Archaeology for 1971, vol. **32**, pt. 2, pp. 168-192.
Some constables' returns, some copies. Some
include exempt poor. Not indexed.
Association Oath Roll, **1696. Ipswich** (by parish),
East Anglian Miscellany, vols. 3 and 4 (1909-10).

Public Record Office [E.179]

Free and Voluntary Present, 1661-2
County [257/7] (5,000).

Hearth Tax *(Assessments and returns)*

1662 (Dec). **Blything hd.** [257/9] (500). Constables'
returns, paper.
(1662). Ipswich, St. Stephen [257/8] (50).
Constables' return, paper.
1663L&M. Bosmere and Claydon and **Plomesgate**
hds. [257/10] (133). Constables' paper returns, for
Aldburgh (54, non-payers?), Rendham (1), Bram-
ford (61, payers), Bosmere and Claydon (17).
1663L. Ipswich St. Peter [257/10a] (103).
Constable's paper return.
1663M. County [257/15] (?5,000). Paper returns of
constables.
(1664). County [257/12] (25,000). Some decay,
repaired, some fading. Exempt poor shown. Brief
introduction and contents list by CAFM.
1663-4 [358]. Miscellaneous constables' paper
returns, unsorted.
1665L. Ipswich [257/13] (750). Paper book,
annotated, exempt poor shown. VG.
1666L. County [183/616] (?5,000). Paper books,
constables' returns. VG.
1670M. [183/605] (200). Fragments, including
Buers, Chilton, Loes hd. (decayed). 2ms.
Adequate legibility and condn.
1674L. County [257/14]. *Published.* Decay to 1m.
repaired.
No date. County [183/610] (2,750). All ms. decayed
in parts, but legibility and condition otherwise
adequate to good.
County [257/17] (6,400). Mostly good condition
and legibility, but some decay, not repaired.
Exempt poor shown.
County [257/18] (?500). Condition too bad to
examine in detail. Not repaired.
County [183/612] (?1,000). Miscellaneous
collection, needing sorting. Varied condition and
legibilty.
(Exemption certificates)
1670M. Ilketshall St. Andrew [183/600] (15).

Suffolk, *Public Record Office*, continued

Hearth Tax (Arrears)
1663M. County (part) [183/614] (150). Latin.
Hoxne, Hartismere, Wangford, Blything and
Cosford hds. [183/565] (50). Latin.

Subsidies
1663. Babergh hd. [183/508] (250).
Blything hd. [183/563] (350). Some decay.
Bury St. Edmunds [183/564] (85). Flat.
(1663). Risbridge hd. [183/602] (160). Flat.
Thedwastre hd. [257/11] (180). Some decay.
No date. Blackbourn hd. [257/16(1)] (50). Ockley,
Wooton ...eningfield, Nurton. Some decay.

Aid (?)
No date. Hartismere hd. [239/184] (51). Decayed
on one side, affecting place names: ...could,
...ngesett Brockford, ...ke Ashe, ...roome, ...waite;
answers of 5 non-payers.

Association Oath Rolls, 1695-6 [C.213]
[264] **County** (24 parts and hundreds);
[265] **Ipswich**; [266] **Orford**; [267] **Aldborough**;
[268] **Bury St. Edmunds.**

Suffolk Record Office, Ipswich

Hearth Tax
1662M. Blackbourn hd. [HD.1538]. *Published.*

Marriage Tax
1695. Ubbeston [FC 69/A1/1].

Window Tax
1715, for parishes of Stuston, Redgrave, Burgate,
Wyverstone, Thornham Magna, Rishangles,
Thwaite, Thorndon and Occold
[HD 79/AD1/3/9-18].

Suffolk Record Office, Bury St. Edmunds

Marriage Tax
1695. Bury St. Edmunds, par. St. James [5508/1].

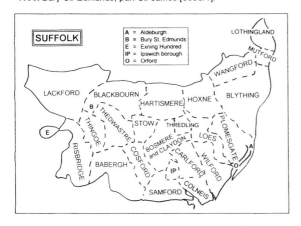

SURREY

Note: Southwark was assessed separately from the
county.

Publications

Free and Voluntary Present 1661-2, for **County**
(excl. Brixton hd. and Southwark) [P.R.O. E.179/
257/28] (3,881), in *Calendar of the Surrey Portion of
the Free and Voluntary Present to Charles II*,
compiled by Cliff Webb, West Surrey Family History
Society Record Series, vol. 2, 1982. Indexed.
Hearth Tax, **1664L, County** (excl. Southwark)
[P.R.O. E.179/188/481] (17,000), in *The Surrey
Hearth Tax, 1664*, ed. C.A.F. Meekings, Surrey
Record Soc., vol. **17**, 1940. Arranged alphabetically.
The introduction includes sample transcripts of
constables' returns and/or exemption certificates for
1662 [P.R.O. E.179/187/479] for **Ripley in Send,
Kennington in Lambeth, Ockham, Woldingham**
and **Wisley**; and for **1664M** [E.179/258/1] for the
east half hd. of **Woking**, for **Send, East** and **West
Horsley, Ockham, East** and **West Clandon,
Ripley in Send,** and **Godalming.**
The introduction has much of relevance
nationally.
Association Oath Rolls for Surrey, 1695,
transcribed by Cliff Webb, West Surrey FHS.
Microfiche Series 3 (one fiche + booklet), 1990.
See also *Surrey Inhabitants Lists*, West Surrey
FHS Research Aid No. 7.

Public Record Office [E.179]

Free and Voluntary Present, **1661-2**
County [257/28] (?5,500). *Published*, except for
Brixton hd. and Southwark.

Hearth Tax (Assessments and returns)

(1662). County [187/479] (many). Paper returns by
constables and exemption certificates. Repaired,
stitched into (?geographical) sections. VG.
1662M-1663L. Lambeth, Prince's and
**Kennington liberties; Battersea,
Merton, Putney, Tooting, Wandsworth, Wimbledon** [257/29] (?4,000).
Constables' paper returns, bound into
book form, easy to use. VG.
**1663. Brixton, Elmbridge, Godalming,
Godley, Tandridge, Wotton** and
Woking hds. with **Guildford** and
Carshalton [257/30] (?10,000).
Constables' paper returns; loose
sheets in six folders, by hd., etc.
Farley [256/29] (8). Constable's
return.
(1663). Bermondsey (pt.), **Bisley,
Crowhurst, Worplesdon** [258/5]
(200). Paper returns from constables.
Also includes Burham, Weeke, West
End tithings.

Surrey: *Public Record Office*, Hearth Tax contd.

1664L. County [188/481]. *Published.*
Blackheath, Brixton, Copthorne, Farnham, Godley, Godalming, Reigate, Tandridge, Wallington, Wotton and **Woking** hds. [258/1] (?20,000). Constables' paper returns and exemption certificates, bound as book. VG.
1664. Leatherhead area [SP.28/1/177; *not* in class E.179].
(1664M-65M). Southwark [258/7] (2,500). Paper book.
Reigate [258/8] (500). Fragments, 2ms. only. 1m. decayed, not repaired, the other OK.
(1664-6). Southwark: St. Olave (part), Upper Ground liberty, **St. Saviour:** Clinke liberty; **Newington; Bermondsey; Lambeth** (first page missing); **West Brixton half hd.; Wandsworth** (these contained the major part of **Southwark and Brixton** hd.); and hds. of **Blackheath, Copthorne and Effingham, Elmbridge, Farnham, Godley, Kingston, Reigate, Tandridge, Wallington** and **Woking** [258/4] (?25,000). Returns by constables, in 18 paper books. Some decay, repaired. VG.
Southwark St. George [188/506] (650). Paper book, annotated, listed by street. VG.
1665L. Brixton hd. [188/489a] (7,500). Annotated list. Considerable decay, repaired.
1666L. Brixton hd. [188/489b] (500). Considerable decay, poor legibility, but some OK and legible.
(1672-3). County [188/504] (15,000). Some decay.
1672-3. County [188/494] (750). Paper exemption certificates.
(1673-4). County [188/496] (15,000). Exchequer duplicate. Double columns.
Woking hd. [258/6] (800). Constable's return, paper book, annotated.
(Arrears)
(1662M-1663M). County and **Southwark** [374/1-3] (1,000). Desperate.
1664. Southwark [188/485] (50).
1670. County [188/508] (?1,000). Draft paper schedule.

Subsidies
(1663). Guildford with **Farnham, Godalming, Godley, Blackheath, Woking** and **Wotton** hds. [188/480] (600). Considerable decay, repaired, but much lost.
(1664). Elmbridge hd. [187/476] (80). Some decay, fading. poor leg.
Kingston hd. [188/484] (100). In bad condition, partly repaired.
(1667) Southwark [272/38] (70). Flat.

Poll Tax
(1677). County [188/502] (?250-500). Exemptions and arrears only.
1689. Southwark, St. George [258/3] (26). Certificate of defaulters.

Surrey, *Public Record Office,* continued

Aid (?)
No date. County [188/505] (?1,000). Fragments, badly decayed, repaired, and faded.

Association Oath Rolls, 1695-6 [C.213]
[269] **County;** [270a-270b] **Deputy Lieuts.** and **Southwark;** [271] **Bletchingley;** [272] **Reigate;** [273] **Gatton;** [274] **Kingston on Thames.** Whole county *published.*

Surrey Record Office, *Kingston upon Thames*

Poll Tax
Leatherhead and Pachenesham liberty, late 17th century [212/66/7].

Kingston Borough Archives, *c/o Surrey R.O.*

Poll Tax
Walton on Thames (incl. Hersham), **1666** [KS1/1/1].

Guildford Muniment Room, *Surrey Record Office*

Hearth Tax
1680. Ash, persons excused [parish register, PSH/AS/1/3];
n.d.? Guildford, Abbot's Hospital, warrant incl. exemptions on grounds of poverty [LM 1047/36].

Subsidy, 1671
Assessment for Artington, Binscombe, Catteshall, Chiddingfold, Compton, Eashing, Farncombe, Godalming town, Guildford (St. N.), Hambledon. Haslemere, Hurtmore, Laborne, Peper Harow, Shackleford, Thursley, Tuesley and Witley (all West Surrey) [Loseley MSS.1506/1-18]. Some in bad condition.

For **Southwark**, see also under **LONDON**.

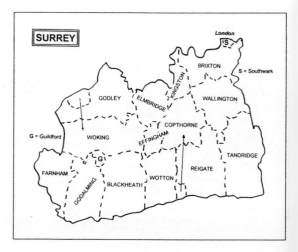

SUSSEX

Note. The Cinque Ports (Winchelsea, Hastings, Rye) were assessed separately. See under Kent.

Publications

Hearth Tax, **1670L** [P.R.O. E.179/191/410] (531), **Chichester** city only, in *Sussex Archaeological Collections*, vol. **24**, 1872, pp. 78-84, transcribed by W.D. Cooper. Not indexed.
Hearth Tax, **1662M, Lewes Rape** [based on 1664M, P.R.O. E.179/258/15] (2,000); **Pevensey Rape** [based on 1665M, E.179/258/16] (2,500), in *Sussex Hearth Tax Assessments 1662.* 1. *Lewes Rape;* 2. *Pevensey Rape*, both ed. M.J. Burchall, introduction in Part **1** by J.H. Farrant, Sussex Genealogical Centre, Occasional Papers Nos. 3 and 4, 1980. Not indexed.
Aid, **Rye, 1660** [E.S.R.O. RYE 82/82] (670), in *The Sussex Genealogist*, vol. **4**, no. 3, pp.97-108.

Public Record Office [E.179]

Hearth Tax (Assessments and returns)
(those available on microfilm from P.R.O. marked §; copies of P.R.O. holdings are at *East Sussex R.O.*)

1664M. Bramber rape [258/14] (2,000). Paper book.
Lewes rape [258/15 §] (2,000). Paper book. *Published.*
(?1664). [191/416 §] (1,500). Fragments, badly decayed but well repaired and now easy to use. Various locations, some identified.
1664-5. Hastings rape [258/20 §] (700). Paper book, repaired. Annotated.
1665M. Pevensey rape [258/16 §] (2,500). Paper book. *Published.*
Pevensey rape [258/19 §] (450). Paper book, annotated. ? if partial duplicate of 258/16.

Public Record Office, Hearth Tax, **1665M** contd.

Bramber rape [258/17 §] (3,350). Nine paper books, annotated.
Lewes rape [258/18 §] (3,600). Twelve paper books, annotated.
1670L. County [191/410 §] (?10,-15,000). In six parts, sewn at head. Much fading and decay, repaired. Notes by CAFM.
No date. Hastings rape [258/21 §] (1,250). Paper book, annotated.

Subsidies

(1664). Lewes rape [191/409] (300). Bad decay, repaired.
No date. Chichester rape [191/412] (?1,000). Decayed, repaired, at head of roll. Roll stitched head to foot. Variable legibility.

Poll Tax

1660. Rye [258/13] (500). Parchment book. By ward, occupation given. VG. Probably a duplicate of Rye Corporation Papers 82/82, see below.

Association Oath Rolls, **1695-6** [C.213]
(Microfilm of C.213/275-283 at *West Sussex R.O.*)

[275] **West Sussex;** [276] **East Sussex;**
[277] Grand Inquest; [278] **Chichester;**
[279] **Midhurst;** [280] **New Shoreham;**
[281] **Bramber;** [282] **Arundel;** [283] **Rye;**
[332] **Cinque Ports.**

West Sussex Record Office, *Chichester*

Microfilm of *Association Oath Rolls* for Sussex [MF 710][P.R.O. C.213/275-283].

Centre for Kentish Studies, *Maidstone*

Poll Tax **1666.** Frant [Powell MSS, U934].

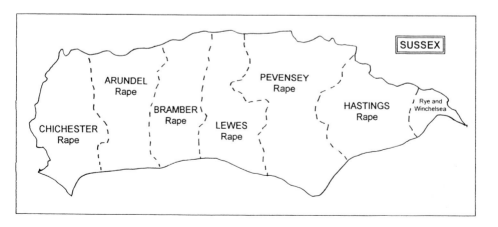

Sussex continued

| **East Sussex Record Office,** Lewes |

Hearth Tax

All P.R.O. Hearth Tax holdings listed, except for E.179/258/14, are on microfilm at E.S.R.O.

Poll Tax
1702-on. Hastings rape. Ashburnham, Beckley, Brightling, Catsfield, Crowhurst, Dallington, Etchingham, Fairlight, Guestling, Hastings (Castle outbounds only), Herstmonceux, Iden, Mountfield, Ninfield, Northiam, Peasmarsh, Penhurst, Pett, Playden, St. Leonards, Salehurst, Udimore, Warbleton, Westfield, Whatlington (1,875) ['with early land tax assessments']. See East Sussex Land Tax, p. xv.

Window Tax
1713. Seaford [SEA 644] (31).

Rye Corporation archives (at E.S.R.O.) include **Hearth Tax** papers:
1662M. Assessment [83/1].
1663. Account of hearths [83/2-4].
1664. Assessment [83/5].
1665. Exemption certificates [83/6-11].

Aid (?). 1660. Rye [Corpn papers 82/82]. Published.

WARWICKSHIRE

Note: Coventry was assessed separately from the County.

Publications

Hearth Tax, **1662M-1674, Hemlingford hd., Tamworth** and **Atherstone divisions** [all relevant P.R.O. and Warwickshire R.O. references for this period] (?3,000), in Warwick County Records, Hearth Tax Returns, vol. **1**, ed. Margaret Walker, 1957/8. Names from all available returns collated. Fully indexed. An immensely detailed introduction by Philip Styles reveals the complexity of the collections under different authorities and of giving these precise dates. Unfortunately no further volumes in this series appeared, and any further transcription done at that stage is not available to the public. However, the Warwickshire County Record Office does have an index to the 1674 return, see above right.

Warwickshire, Publications continued

Hearth Tax, **1663** [Warwickshire R.O., Q.S.11/5], for Farnborough, Warmington, Mollington, Wormleighton, Shotteswell, Avon and Burton Dassett, Fenny Compton, Priors Hardwick and Ratley (420), transcribed by J.S.W. Gibson, in Cake and Cockhorse (Banbury Historical Society), vol. **1**, 1960, pp. 45-48, 62-64, 78-79. Indexed.
Hearth Tax, **1662, 1671, Tysoe** [Warwickshire R.O., Q.S. 11/2, 11/?] in The Parish Registers of Tysoe, ed. D.B. Woodfield, 1976. Indexed.
Poll Tax, **1660**, Knowle [location of original now unknown] (77) in Records of Knowle, 1914, 379-80.

Index (in Warwickshire Record Office)
Hearth Tax 1674 (10,000). Whole county.

| **Public Record Office** [E.179] |

Free and Voluntary Present, 1661-2
County [259/7] (?15,000).
Microfilm at Warwickshire County Record Office.
Coventry [194/326] (349). Part arranged by ward.
MS transcript at Coventry City Record Office.

Hearth Tax (assessments and returns)
(those available on microfilm from P.R.O. marked §: microfilm or photostat copies of returns for 1664-5, 1666L, 1671M, 1673M and 1679-80 are at Warwickshire County Record Office.)

1664M-1665M?. County (including Coventry) [259/10 §] (17,170). Annotated. Mostly in good condition, but a few ms. faded. Part published. [Styles' introduction, pp. 42-44].
1666L. County (including Coventry) [259/9] (15,670). Paper book, annotated, forges, ovens, shown. VG. Part published [Styles' introduction p. 58].
1671M. Hemlingford hd. [194/325 §] (3,500). Considerable decay, repaired, and variable legibility [Styles' introduction, p.70]. Includes the greater part of the Birmingham division, missing from the county copy. Partly published.
Knightlow hd. [194/338 §] (?1,500). Much decayed, repaired.
1673M. Hemlingford and Kington hds. [259/12 §] (1,250). Badly decayed, repaired. Notes by CAFM.
(1679-80). Coventry, Fillongley and Coleshill [259/11 §] (800). Paper, repaired. Annotated. see The Hearth Tax Collectors' Book for Worcester 1678-1680, ed. C.A.F. Meekings, S. Porter and I. Roy, Worcs. Hist. Soc. N.S. vol. **11**, 1983, Introduction, page 12.
1683/4. Birmingham [375/1] (243). Newly erected and smiths' hearths, in Birmingham (by street), Erdington, Edgbaston, Bordesley, Castle Bromwich, Derrit End and Little Bromwich. VG. [Styles' introduction, p.97].

Warwickshire, *Public Record Office* continued

Hearth Tax (Arrears and exemption certificates)
1662M. County [259/6 §] (?500). Desperate
arrears, in Latin.
Coventry [194/329] (?1,500). Includes long lists
for Coventry. Parchment and paper.
1663M. County [374/4,5] (125). Sperate and
desperate. [Styles, introduction, p. 28].
1662-66. County and Coventry [194/327 §] (?150).
Varied legibility, some annotations [many
references in Styles' introduction].
(Exemption certificates)
(1671-2). County [194/334 §] (?2,000). Fragile.
1671-74. County [347] [Styles, page 70].

Subsidies
1663. Coventry [259/8] (250). By street.
1663/4. Coventry [194/330] (171). By ward.
Transcript at *Coventry C.R.O.*
(1663). Hemlingford hd. [194/328] (?500).
Considerable decay, repaired, but some parts
legible (includes Solihull).

Association Oath Rolls, 1695-6 [C.213]
[284-85] **County;** [286] **Coventry;** [287] **Warwick;**
[288] **Stratford.**

| **Warwickshire County Record Office.** |

Free and Voluntary Present, 1661-2. Microfilm of
P.R.O. E.179/259/7.

Hearth Tax

TS index of **1674** return.
Photostats of P.R.O. returns for **1664-5** and **1666L**
[E.179/259/10,9]; *microfilm* of P.R.O. returns for
1671, 1673, 1679-80 [E.179/325,338, 259/12,11].

Original returns:
1662M. County [Q.S.11/1–4] (8,850). Part
published. Part of Atherstone and all Birmingham
missing [Styles, pp.16-17].
1664L. County [Q.S.11/5] (15,376). Part *published*
[Styles, pp.30-31].
[The following returns, **1670-1674**, are referenced
Q.S. 11/7-59, consisting of 53 separate books.
Part *published.* Styles' introduction, pages 69-75.]
1670 (1669M-1670M). **County** (16,770).
1671 (1671L-1671M). **Kineton hd; Hemlingford
hd.,** Solihull, Tamworth, Atherstone divns (7,230).
1673 (1672L-1673L). **County** (16,560).
1674 (1673M-1674L). **County** (16,420). Indexed.
1682-4. New hearths and forges, in **Birmingham,
Deritend, Edgbaston,** liberties of **Aston**
[Q.S.11/60-63] [Styles' introduction, page 97].

Poll Tax
Wellesbourne Hastings, **1678** [CR133/81].
Chilvers Coton, **1690** [CR 136/?]

Aid
**1692/3. Hemlingford hd.: Atherstone and
Tamworth divns.** [CR136/C1646] (1,700).

Warwickshire *County Record Office* continued

Marriage Tax
Fenny Compton, **1698** [DR 103/7]. See 'A Census of
a Warwickshire village in 1698', Philip Styles,
Birmingham Hist. Jnl. 3, 33-51.

Window Tax
1700-1738. Brailes [DR 308/147/1-10].
1708-1737. Hartshill [N2/570-89].

Land Tax
Hampton in Arden: Balsall, **1711** [CR 112/Ba
1456,148].
Wellesbourne Hastings, **1711** [CR 133/82] (25).

| **Coventry City Record Office** |

Transcripts of the *Free and Voluntary Present,*
1661-2 [P.R.O. E.179/194/326] (349) and the
Subsidy, **1663/4** [P.R.O. E.179/194/330] (171),
both of Coventry only.

| **Shakespeare Birthplace Trust Records Office,**
Stratford upon Avon. |

Hearth Tax
Photocopies of returns for 1662, 1663, 1670, 1673,
1674 [PR 72] [presumably from *W.C.R.O.* Q.S.11].

Aids, Subsidies etc (originals)
Alveston, **1668** [DR 74/21].
Fillongley, **1690, 1692** [ER 65/21,22].
Stivichall, *subsidy,* **1671-2** [DR 10/1842].

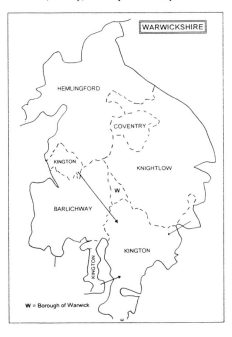

W = Borough of Warwick

WESTMORLAND

Publications

Hearth Tax, **1670M, County** [P.R.O. E.179/ 195/73] (5,000) and **1663, Kendal** only [E.179/ 195/74] (100), in *Records Relating to the Barony of Kendale*, vols. **1** and **2**, by William Farrer and/or John F. Curwen (1923 and 1924), and *The Later Records relating to North Westmorland*, by J.F. Curwen (1932), also published by the Cumberland and Westmorland Antiquarian and Archaeological Society, Records Series vols. **4**, **5** and **8**. These volumes consist of miscellaneous abstracts of a variety of records, arranged by parish, but each parish entry includes the 1670M Hearth Tax, with Kendal additionally having that for 1663. Indexed.

Public Record Office [E.179]

Hearth Tax

(1663). Kendal ward [195/74] (100). Badly decayed, not repaired. *Published.*
1662M-1664L. County [259/13] (?500). Returns of defaulters. Includes original constables' paper returns, and enrolled parchment copies in Latin.
1670M. County [195/73] (5,000). *Published.* Flat, short ms., some fading.
No date. County [259/14] (3,500). Flat, short ms., some decay, much fading.

Association Oath Rolls, 1695-6 [C.213] [289] **Appleby;** [290] **Kirkby in Kendal.**
See also Cumberland rolls, page 20.

Cumbria Record Office, Kendal

Hearth Tax (original)
1674. County, excluding Kendal [WD/Ry Box 28]. A notebook of Sir Daniel Fleming.

Marriage Tax
1695. Lists of inhabitants for parishes in **Lonsdale ward,** and Highgate, Stramongate and Stricklandgate in the town of **Kendal** [WD/Ry Box 32]. Indexed.

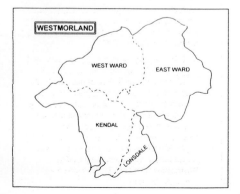

WILTSHIRE

Publications

'Salisbury: A Royal Aid and Supply for 1667' (*Wiltshire Arch. & Natural History. Soc. Mag.* **36,** pp. 413-34, indexed). Reprinted in *Endless Street: A History of Salisbury,* J. Chandler, 1983.
'Association Oath Rolls' for Wiltshire', signatories. *Wilts N&Q* **6** (1908-10), pp. 197-201, 349-51, 485-492. See also **7** (1911-13), pp. 42-43.
Surviving *North Wiltshire 1695 Tax Censuses* [Marriage Tax] (2 parts).

Public Record Office [E.179]

Hearth Tax *(Assessments and returns)*

1662M. County [259/29] (11,000). In four parts, ms. sewn at top, flat. Much decay, repaired, and fading. The only full return for the county.
(Exemption certificates)
1662M. County [259/26b] (1,000). Paper certificates from constables, bound into book. In good condition.
  County [374/6] (120). Enrolment on parchment of 259/26b. Latin.
1673/4. [360]. Miscellaneous.
(Arrears)
1662M. County [374/7] (120). Latin.
1671M. Malmesbury, Chippenham and **Calne hds.** [199/424] (50). Decayed but repaired and now in good condition and legible.

Subsidies
1663. Dunworth, Mere and **South Damerham hds.** [199/420] (?500). Mostly badly decayed, repaired, and bad legibility. Only 1m. reasonably OK.
1663/4. Warminster, Heytesbury, Whorwellsdown hds. and **liberty of Deverill Longbridge** (part of Damerham South hd.) [199/421] (500). Slight decay and some fading on some ms., generally OK.
1664. Underditch, Downton, Cawden and Cadworth, Frustfield, Branch and Dole and **Chalke hds.** [259/27] (450). Good.

Poll Tax
1660. Whorwellsdown hd. [259/26a] (96). Some decay at foot (? if Poll Tax).
(1660). Salisbury [199/419] (2,000). Arranged by street. Some fading on final m., otherwise VG.
  Salisbury Close [199/416] (180). Flat.
  Bradford hd. [199/418] (200). Flat ms. Half very faded, part OK. (? if Poll Tax).
No date. [259/28] (100). Boyton and Corton, Horningsham (decayed and faded), Boreham, Bishopstrowe, Norton Bavent.

Wiltshire: *Public Record Office* continued

Association Oath Rolls, 1695-6 [C.213]
See *publications.*
[291] **County**; [292] Militia Officers; [293] **New Sarum** (Salisbury); [294] **Wilton**; [295] **Downton**; [296] **Hindon**; [297] **Westbury**; [298] **Calne**; [299] **Devizes**; [300] **Chippenham**; [301] **Malmesbury**; [302] **Great Bedwin**; [303] **Ludgershall**; [304] **Marlborough**; [305] **Ramsbury**; [306] **Bradford**.

Wiltshire Record Office, Trowbridge

Marriage Tax [212B/7202A/1-16]
(There are transcripts for asterisked returns at the *Wiltshire R.O.*; see also *publications,* left.)

[1] Broad Hinton, Binknoll tithing only, 1697, 1700, 1701; [2] Chisledon, 1697; [3] Chisledon with Draycot Foliatt, 1700*, 1702, 1705; [4] Cliffe Pypard 1697, 1701*; [5] Hilmarton (except Catcomb tithing) 1697*, 1700, 1701*; [6] Liddington, 1697, 1700, 1702; [7] Lydiard Tregoze, 1697, 1700, 1701; [8] Lyneham 1697*, 1700, 1701, 1702; [9] Swindon 1697*, 1701, 1702, 1705; [10] Tockenham 1697, 1700, 1701;

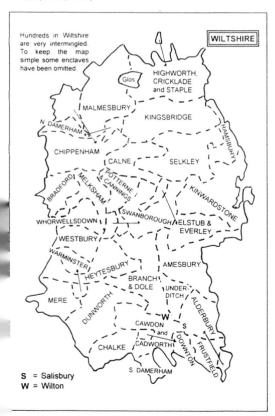

Hundreds in Wiltshire are very intermingled. To keep the map simple some enclaves have been omitted.

WILTSHIRE

S = Salisbury
W = Wilton

Wiltshire Record Office, Marriage Tax continued

[11] Wanborough 1697, 1700, 1702, 1705*; [12] Wootton Bassett 1697*, 1701*, 1702, 1705; [13] Little Hinton 1700 [14] Wroughton (incl. the five tithings in Kingsbridge) 1700, 1701*; [15] Wroughton (incl. town tithing only) 1697; [16] Wroughton (Elcombe and Ufcott tithings only) 1705. **1695.** Donhead St. Mary [980/2].

Window Tax
1704-1740. City of **Salisbury**, in four wards [G23/1/188-191] (600 each year).

Salisbury city records:
Aid: **1667. Salisbury** [G. 23/1/172]. *Published,* see left.

WORCESTERSHIRE

Note: Worcester was assessed separately from the County.

Publications

The Hearth Tax Collectors' Book for Worcester, 1678-1680, ed. C. Meekings, S. Porter and I. Roy, Worcestershire Hist. Soc., N.S. vol. **11**, 1983 [P.R.O. E.179/260/13(1)] (2,301). Indexed. Informative introduction which discusses the administrative records for both city and county.

Bromsgrove and the Poll Tax of 1690, transcribed from notes of W.A. Cotton (1908) by Alan Broomfield, published by Birmingham & Midland Society for Genealogy & Heraldry (1993). Original notes at Birmingham Reference Library, location of original documents unknown.

Public Record Office [E.179]

Hearth Tax (Assessments and returns) (those available on microfilm from P.R.O. marked §; copies of all Hearth Tax records are at the *Wiltshire R.O.*).

1662M. County (excl. Worcester) [201/325 §] (?9,000). Flat ms. sewn at top, considerable decay at feet of ms. repaired, and staining and fading, poor legibility. **County** (prob. excl. Worcester) [260/4 §] (many). Constables' paper returns, well repaired and bound in book form. **1664L. County** (excl. Worcester) [260/16 §] (?5,000). Repaired but badly decayed and faded. Introduction by CAFM. **Worcester** [201/323 §]. Decayed and mainly illegible.

Worcestershire, P.R.O., Hearth Tax, continued

1664M-1665M (revision of **1662M**). County (excl. Worcester) [201/312 §] (10,000). Enrolled. Some decay, part repaired, fading and staining, but much OK. Exempt poor shown. Intro. by CAFM. **Worcester** [260/8 §] (890). Annotated. By ward.
1666L. County (excl. Worcester) [260/5 §] (4,500); [260/6 §] (3,000).
1671L. County (excl. Worcester) [260/9 §] (7,500). Much decay (repaired) and fading. Poor condition.
(?1671-2). County (excl. Worcester) [375/15 §] (5,000). Considerable decay, repaired, variable legibility but mostly OK. Brief introduction.
1673L. Worcester [260/12 §] (1,000). Ms. sewn head to foot. Annotated. Some fading and damage.
1674L. County [260/10 §] (11,500).
Worcester [260/11 §] (1,024). Ms. sewn head to foot. Annotated as 260/12.
1679M-1680M (based on **1678** assessment).
Worcester [260/13(1) §] (2,301). *Published.*
Worcester [260/13(2) §]. Consists of some loose paper leaves (150 names). Not clear if these are included in the published volume.
Kidderminster [260/14 §] (500). Paper book, VG. See *Worcester Hearth Tax*, Introduction, page 12.
(Arrears and exemption certificates)
1662M. County [374/8-10 §] (275). Latin, constables', sperate and desperate.
1663L. Worcester [374/12] (?75). Latin. Sperate.
1663M. County [201/317/2,3 §; 374/11 §] (400). Latin. Constables' sperate, desperate.
Worcester [260/7 §] (?250). Desperate.

Public Record Office, Hearth Tax continued

1663L&M. County [201/317/1 §] (very many). Paper exemption certificates, repaired and bound in two volumes.
1663-4. County [201/318a §]. Latin, 1664 (750). English, exemption certificates, annotated, 1663-4 (550).

Subsidies
1660. County [260/3*] (1,000). Decay at feet of some ms. Part of Poll Tax ?
1663. Halfshire hd. [201/322] (250).
Pershore hd. [201/319] (400).
(1663). Doddingtree hd. [201/315a] (300). Some decay, repaired. Considerable fading/staining, legibility variable.
1664. Doddingtree hd. [201/320] (300).
Worcester [201/321] (130).
(1664). Evesham [201/307] (44). Some decay, repaired, but most names survive.

Poll Tax
1660. Worcester [270/21] (3,000). Paper, well repaired and bound together, easy to use (photocopy at *County R.O.*)
County [274/10] (?500-1,000). Paper. Includes: North and Middle Littleton, Great and Little Hampton, Badsey, Offenham, Aldington, Bratforton, Evesham St. Lawrence, Weckhamford, Littleton, Dengworth, Evesham All Saints, Lenchwick and Norton.

Association Oath Rolls, 1695-6 [C.213]
[307] **County;** [308] **Worcester;** [309] **Droitwich;** [310] **Evesham;** [311] **Bewdley;** [312] **Kidderminster.**

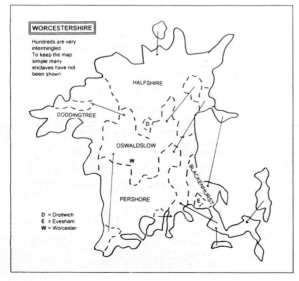

```
WORCESTERSHIRE
Hundreds are very
intermingled.
To keep the map
simple many
enclaves have not
been shown

HALFSHIRE

DODDINGTREE
              D
OSWALDSLOW
              W
                    BLACKENHURST
PERSHORE
                    E

D = Droitwich
E = Evesham
W = Worcester
```

> ### Hereford and Worcester Record Office at *County Hall, Spetchley Road, Worcester.*
>
> ### Hearth Tax
> **1662M. Doddingtree hd.** [In Midsummer 1662 Quarter Sessions, packet no.102, Documents nos. 1-33]. Constables' returns for 33 places.

> ### At *Worcester Branch, St. Helen's, Fish Street, Worcester.*
>
> Microfilm of all Worcesterhire and Worcester *Hearth Tax* Records at the P.R.O.
> Photocopy of the *Poll Tax*, **1660**, for **Worcester** [P.R.O. E.179/270/21]

> ### Birmingham Central Library, Archives Division
>
> *Poll Tax.* Bromsgrove.
> See *publications*, page 63.

YORKSHIRE

Publications

Hearth Tax: Transcripts of the whole of Yorkshire for 1672-3 have already been published or will be by the end of 1996. These are detailed under York and the three Ridings.

Public Record Office [C.213]

Association Oath Rolls, 1695-6
[313] **Yorkshire;** [314] **Yorkshire** (35 items). These two references probably relate to all three Ridings.

YORK

Publications

Hearth Tax. 1672L. **York** *City parishes and the Wapentake of the **Ainsty*** [York City Archives, E80]. Ripon HS and Ripon, Harrogate & Dist FHS, 1992 (see North Riding). Indexed.
'York in the 17th Century' by G.C.F. Forster, in *V.C.H.: City of York*, pp. 162-5 (discussion only).

Public Record Office [E.179]

Hearth Tax (Assessments and returns)

1665. City and Ainsty [260/20] (?2,500).
1671M. City [260/21] (2,000). Ms. sewn at head.
1672. City [260/22] (2,124). Imperfect. Contents list by CAFM.
No date. City [260/23] (84). Fragment. Acombe, Acaster, Malbis, Acaster Selby.
(Arrears) (see also page 70)
(1663). City [270/52] (700). Latin.
1664. City and Ainsty [218/211] (550). Latin.

Subsidy
(1664). Ainsty [218/215] (100).

Association Oath Roll, 1695 [C.213]
[316] **York.**

York City Archives, York

Hearth Tax
1665. York and Ainsty [M30:22/23].
1670. York [M30:24]; **Ainsty** [E.80a].
1672. York [E80]. (1,800). *Published.*
Ainsty [M30:25]. *Published.*
1674. York and Ainsty [M30:26].

Subsidy Rolls etc. (all **York**)
1665. Micklegate ward [M30:5].
1690. Micklegate, Monk wards [M30:6-7].
1691. Bootham, Micklegate, Walmgate, Monk wards [M30:8-14].
1692. Walmgate ward [M30:15].
1693. St. Wilfrid's parish [M30.16].

York: *York City Archives* continued

Poll Tax
1690. York and Ainsty [M30:20,21].
1695-6. York, St. Martin Coney parish only (also described as 'Land Tax') [M30:31].
No date. *c.*1694. **York,** Christ's Parish and Minster Yard with Bedern [M30:30].

Association Oath Roll, **1695-6**
Council, gentry, clergy, citizens of **York** [M30:32].

Window Tax
1701. York, 19 parishes [K96] (650).

YORKSHIRE: EAST RIDING

Note: Kingston upon Hull was assessed separately from the County.

Publications

Hearth Tax: **1672L, East Riding** [P.R.O. E.179/205/504] and **1673L Kingston upon Hull** [E.179/205/505], from microfilm at *Humberside A.O.* and *Kingston upon Hull C.R.O.* To be published, 1996. in three parts, by Ripon HS and Ripon, Harrogate & Dist FHS (see North Riding).
Marriage Tax, **1695, 1697, Hull** [Hull C.R.O. CAT.91-99] in *The People of Hull in 1695 and 1697:* An index to the poll tax assessments (not in fact a poll tax), K.H.C. R.O. and East Yorks FHS, 1990. 1695 excluding Humber ward. 1697 excluding St. Mary's and North wards.

Public Record Office [E.179]

Free and Voluntary Present, **1661-2**
Holderness wap. [205/513] (750).

Hearth Tax (Assessments and returns)
(those available on microfilm from P.R.O. marked §: all, except 205/18, available at *Humberside A.O.*)

1662-3. Holderness (mainly) [261/4 §] (?1,500). Miscellaneous paper returns from constables.
(?1664). East Riding [261/5 §] (?1,500). Considerable decay, not repaired, also fading. Hull [205/499 §] (1,200).
(1667). East Riding [205/501 §] (3,000). Increases and decreases of taxable hearths. Some decay, repaired, some fading.
(1670). East Riding [205/514 §] (17,000). Slight decay at edges, not repaired. Includes exempt poor.
1672. East Riding [205/504 §] (15,000). Loose ms.. formerly sewn at head. Occasional decay, repaired. For *publication.*
1673L. Hull [205/505 §] (1,500). Some decay, not repaired, mostly OK. For *publication.*
1673-74. Ten paper books, all VG, annotated and showing exempt poor:
1673. Holderness wap. [205/518] (1,500).

65

Yorkshire: East Riding, *P.R.O. Hearth Tax* contd.

1673M & 1674L. Harthill wap. [205/519 §] (1,050).
1674. Holderness wap. [205/520 §] (1,150).
1674L. Dickering wap. [205/521 §] (2,000).
1673M & 1674L. Buckrose wap. [205/522 §] (2,000).
1673M & 1674L. Harthill wap., Bainton Beacon [205/523 §] (1,150).
prob. 1674. Harthill wap., Hunsley Beacon [205/524] (1,250). Some pages fragile.
prob. 1674. Beverley [205/525 §] (650).
1674L. Harthill wap., Howdenshire [261/9 §] (900).
1673M & 1674L. Ouse and Derwent wap. (with **Hull**) [261/10 §] (1,500).
1675. East Riding [261/11 §] (?15,000).

(Arrears) (see also page 70)
1663. East Riding [205/493 §] (200) and [205/495] (450).
1664. Hull [261/6 §] (200). By ward.
1665M. East Riding [205/502] (5,000).

Subsidies
1663. Harthill wap., Holme Beacon [205/492] (50). Badly decayed fragment, repaired, legibility variable.
(1664). Hull [205/494] (225).
Holderness wap. [205/497] (?150). Badly decayed, repaired, but most names lost, and legibility poor.
Harthill wap., Howdenshire [205/498] (150).
Harthill wap., Bainton Beacon [205/467] (150).

Yorkshire: East Riding, *P.R.O.* continued

Poll Tax or Aids
(1660). Hull [205/486] (1,250). Mainly OK, but 1m. faded.
Holderness wap. [205/487] (750). Ms. sewn end to end.
Holderness wap. [205/488] (1,000). VG.
Hull, Humber ward [205/489] (300).
Hull, Austin ward [205/490] (750).
Hull [205/460] (250). Variable legibility.
1667. East and West Ridings [261/7] (?500-1,000). Schedules of defaulters. Two bundles. ms. of varying size.
(1667) Hull, Trinity Ward [205/484] (700). VG. Microfilm at *Humberside A.O.*

Association Oath Rolls, 1695-6 [C.213]
[317-18] **Hull;** [323] **Hedon;** [330] **Holderness.**
See also under 'Yorkshire', page 65.

Humberside Archive Office, *Beverley*

Microfilm available of P.R.O. holdings of *Hearth Tax* Returns, except for E.179/205/518; also of *Subsidy,* **Hull, 1677** [E.179/205/484].

Kingston upon Hull City Record Office

Free and Voluntary Present,
1661-2 [CAT.35] for all town.

Aids etc.
1661. Disbanding forces [CAT.37-42]. All town.
1677. [CAT.43-44]. One ward of town, two townships in county.
1678. [CAT.45-46]. Five wards of town, five townships in county.
1678/9. [CAT.57-67]. Five wards of town, six townships in county.
1679/80. [CAT.68-75]. Four wards of town, four townships in county.
1689/92. [CAT. 76-90]. Each year, some town wards only.

Marriage Tax [CAT.91-99]
1695, 1697. *Published.*

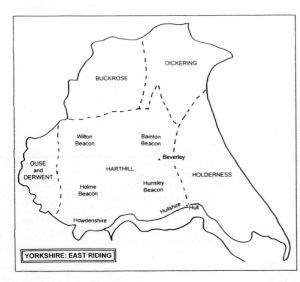

YORKSHIRE: NORTH RIDING

Publications

The Hearth Tax List for the **North Riding** of Yorkshire, **1673M** [P.R.O. E.179/ 216/462] (22,500), ed. John Hebden, published 1991 by Ripon Historical Society and Ripon, Harrogate, & District Family History Group (J.R. Hebden, Aldergarth, Galphay, Ripon, North Yorks. HG4 3NJ). *Indexed.*

1. **Gilling West** and **Hang West Wapentakes** (Richmond, Middleham, Upper Wensleydale, Upper Swaledale, south side of Upper Teesdale).
2. **Allerton, Gilling East, Hallikeld** and **Hang East Wapentakes** (Vale of Mowbray, northern part of Vale of York, including Northallerton, Bedale and Masham).
3. **Birdforth** and **Bulmer Wapentakes** (Thirsk, Easingwold, almost reaches Helmsley and Malton and including some townships now part of York city).
4. **Ryedale, Pickering Lyth** and **Scarborough Wapentakes** (Helmsley, Malton, Pickering, Scarborough and southern part of North York Moors).
5. **Langbarugh West, Langbarugh East Wapentakes** and **Whitby Strand Liberty** (west of Stokesley through Guisborough to Whitby and including northern part of North York Moors).

Hearth Tax **1673** for **Downholme and Walburn** in Hangwest wap. [P.R.O E.179/216/463] (38) in 'The Hearth Tax and other records', by R. Fieldhouse, in *Group Projects in Local History*, A. Rogers, 1977.

Yorkshire: North Riding continued

Public Record Office [E.179]

Hearth Tax (Assessments and returns)

1662M. North Riding [215/451] (22,200).
North Riding [215/452] (22,200). Duplicate of 215/451. Richmond town excluded. Terrington parish [245/20] (62). Paper.
1663L. Bulmer wap. [261/23] (?2,000). Constables' paper returns, variable condition.
(1663). Hallikeld wap. [215/455] (1,200). Includes exempt poor.
1664L. Pickering Lythe wap. [261/27] (?1,000). Constables' paper returns.
(1664). Bulmer wap. [216/458] (8,000). Includes exempt poor.
(1667). North Riding [216/460] (8,250). Increases and decreases.
(?1667). North Riding [216/473] (10,000). Increases and decreases. Parts badly decayed, not repaired, and faded. Poor legibility.
Bulmer, Birdforth, East and West Hang, West Gilling waps., Allertonshire lib. [261/26] (5,000). Much fading, poor legibility.
1670. North Riding [216/461] (32,000). Opening ms. faded, but most OK. Exempt poor shown.
1671. West Gilling wap. [261/28] (250). Papers, bound together.
(?1671). North Riding [261/29] (300). Schedule of variations. Flat. Much decay, not repaired.
pre-1673. Birdforth wap. [261/33] (1,800). Flat.

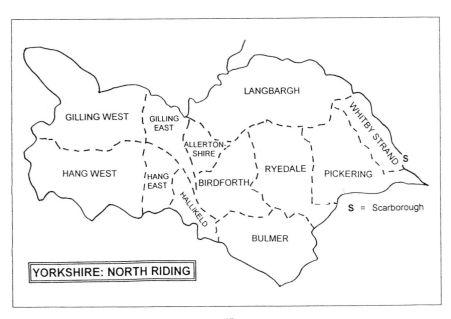

YORKSHIRE: NORTH RIDING

LANGBARGH

GILLING WEST | GILLING EAST

ALLERTON-SHIRE

HANG WEST | HANG EAST | BIRDFORTH | RYEDALE | PICKERING

HALLIKELD

BULMER

WHITBY STRAND

S

S = Scarborough

Yorkshire: North Riding, *P.R.O., Hearth Tax* ctd.

1673M. North Riding [216/462] (22,500). Exempt poor shown. *Published.*
1673-74. Five paper books, all including exempt poor:
  1673. Bulmer wap. [216/481] (3,100).
  1673. Allertonshire lib. [216/482] (1,050).
  1673/4. Ryedale wap. [216/483] (2,250).
  1673M & 1674L. Hallikeld wap. [216/484] (1,025).
  1673. East Gilling wap. [261/30] (1,350).
1674. Birdforth, Hang, West Gilling, Langbaurgh, Pickering Lythe waps. and **Whitby lib.** [261/32] (?8,000). Paper returns by constables, repaired, bound.
(1678). North Riding (part) [216/470] (?250). Schedule of exemptions. Much lost from decay, repaired and fading, but parts are legible.
No date. Allertonshire lib. [216/469] (1,200). Including exempt poor.
East Gilling wap. [216/471] (1,5000). Exempt poor shown.
East Hang wap. [216/472] (1,150). Exempt poor shown.
West Hang wap. [216/474] (2,000). Exempt poor shown.
West Gilling wap. [261/34] (2,700).
Langbaurgh wap. [261/35] (5,000). Exempt poor shown.
Bulmer wap. [249/4]. Huntington only.
(Arrears) (see also page 70).
1663L. North Riding [374/13] (400). Latin. Desperate.

Subsidies
1660. Great Ormsby [239/233] (80). Perhaps Aid, not Subsidy.
(1663). Bulmer wap. [215/453] (350).
Hallikeld wap./Richmondshire [216/457] (100). Variable condition and legibility.
Langbaurgh wap. [261/24] (400).
(1664). Bulmer wap. [215/454] (?150). Badly decayed, repaired; much lost.
Pickering Lythe wap. and **Whitby lib.** [216/465] (55). Some decay and fading.
Allertonshire lib. [261/25] (200).
1673. Scarborough [261/31] (70). ? date.
No date. West Gilling wap. [216/477] (100). Badly decayed and faded.

Association Oath Rolls, **1695-6** [C.213]
[320] **Scarborough**; [322] Richmond; [325] **Thirsk**; [326] **Northallerton.**
See also under 'Yorkshire', page 65.

North Yorkshire County Record Office,
Northallerton

Marriage Tax: Richmond, 1697-1705.
List of actual births, etc., on which tax was paid.

YORKSHIRE: WEST RIDING

Publications

Note. The following publications together cover the whole of the West Riding.
The Hearth Tax List for the **West Riding** *of Yorkshire,* **1672L**, ed. John Hebden, published 1990-94 by Ripon Historical Society and Ripon, Harrogate, and District Family History Group (see North Riding). Indexed. [Parts **2**, **3** and **4** from Wakefield M.D. Library original].
1. **Claro Wapentake** [P.R.O. E.179/210/400] (Ripon, Harrogate, Knaresborough, Wetherby).
2. **Staincliffe and Ewcross Wapentake** (all north west of the West Riding from Keighley in the south to Sedburgh in the north and west to the Lancashire border).
3. **Agbrigg** and **Morley Wapentakes,** 1, *Township Lists;* 2, *Surname Index* (much of the later industrial area: Bradford, Halifax, Huddersfield, suburbs of Leeds, Wakefield etc.).
4. **Barston** [sic] **Ash and Osgoldcross Wapentakes** (Goole, part of Tadcaster, Selsby, Pontefract and Castleford).

The Hearth Tax Returns for South Yorkshire **[Strafforth/Strafford and Tickhill Wapentake, Staincross Wapentake],** *1672L* [from Wakefield M.D. Library original] (7,933), ed. David Hey, publication of the Names Project team at the Centre for English Cultural Tradition and Language and the Division of Continuing Education, University of Sheffield, 1991. Indexed.
'Return of the *Hearth Tax* for the **Wapentake of Skyrack, 1672'** [P.R.O. E.179/210/417], contr. by John Stansfield, *Miscellanea,* Thoresby Soc., vol. **2**. pt. 3, 1891, pp.180-204, Aberforth - Leeds, Kirkgate (2,000), indexed; and vol. **4** pt. 1, 1892, pp.17-36. Leeds, Briggate - Yeadon (1,750), indexed.
Hearth Tax, **Leeds 1663** [Leeds Corporation Court Book, LC/M1 p. 212 foll., Leeds Archives] (1,500) in *The Municipal History of the Borough of Leeds,* by James Wardell, 1846, pp. lxxxii-cxiii. Not indexed.
Hearth Tax, **Knaresborough, Bilton cum Harrogate, Pannall, 1664L** (wrongly described as 1676) [P.R.O. E.179/210/393] in *Records of Harrogate,* ed. Walter J. Kaye, 1922, Appendix 7.
The Hearth Tax Returns of 1672L for the **Wakefield** *Metropolitan District* [from original in Wakefield M.D. Library] (2,500), transcribed by Mrs. J.A. Bottomley and Miss Dorothy Petyt, Wakefield Hist. Soc. Journal, vol. **5**, 1978. Arranged in alphabetical order of township. Original omits Pontefract. Not indexed.
Hearth Tax, **Sheffield, 1665,** and *Poll Tax,* **1692** (also list of smiths and cutlers, 1670) in 'Descent of the Manor of Sheffield', by S.I. Tucker, *Jnl. of the British Archaeologhical Association,* **30**, 1874, pp. 237-77, index at pp. 489-93.

68

Yorkshire: West Riding continued

Public Record Office [E.179]

Hearth Tax (Assessments and returns)
(those available on microfilm from P.R.O. marked §;
returns relating to **Strafforth and Tickhill** wapentake at *Sheffield Record Office.*)

1662M. Ripon lib. [210/386] (1,000). VG.
Leeds borough [262/9] (?1,500). Bad decay, not
repaired. Condition too bad to examine.
1664L. West Riding [210/393 §] (32,000). Includes
exempt poor for Agbrigg, Morley, Staincliffe waps.
1664M. Barkston wap. [210/392] (800).
Supplementary assessment.
1666L. Agbrigg and **Morley waps.** [210/394a]
(8,800). Paper book, VG.
Skyrack wap. [210/421] (4,000). Some decay,
repaired. Includes exempt poor.
Claro wap. [262/11 §] (3,250). Paper book.
1670M. West Riding [210/411] (27,500). Some
decay at feet of ms., repaired.
West Riding [262/12] (1,120). Schedule of empty
houses and certified exempt.
(prob. 1670M). Staincross, Osgoldcross and
Staincliffe waps. [210/414], part of 210/411]
(600). Badly decayed and faded. Not repaired.

(1670). Sheffield [210/396] (350). Sewn head to
foot.
1671. West Riding [210/399] (3,900). Variations in
assessments. Interesting annotations.
1672L (note that the P.R.O. holdings are copies of
the original now held at *Wakefield M.D. Library*
and mostly published).
Claro wap. [210/400] (5,000). Very long ms.
Including exempt poor. *Published.*
Staincliffe wap. [210/418] (5,500). Including
exempt poor.
Strafforth and Tickhill wap. [262/15 §] (5,500).
Very long ms. Microfilm at *Sheffield Central
Library.*
Prob. **1672L.** Barkstone wap. [262/14] (2,500).
(1672). Staincross wap. [210/412] (1,500). Very
long ms.
Agbrigg and **Morley waps.** [210/413] (?20,000).
Osgoldcross wap. [210/415] (?2,500). Not
checked in detail because of bad condition.
Skyrack wap. [210/417] (3,750). Includes exempt
poor. *Published.*
1674L. West Riding [262/13] (35,000).
No date. West Riding [262/17] (?5,000).
Fragments, repaired and stitched into one roll.
Very miscellaneous. Bad condition and legibility.

YORKSHIRE: WEST RIDING

STAINCLIFFE

CLARO

Ainsty of YORK

SKYRACK

BARKSTON ASH

MORLEY

OSGOLDCROSS

AGBRIGG

STAINCROSS

STRAFFORTH and TICKHILL

Yorkshire: West Riding: *P.R.O.* continued

Hearth Tax (Arrears)
1663L. West Riding [210/388b] (900). Some
fading.
1663M. West Riding [210/388a] (800). VG.
1662M-1664L. (1665-6). West Riding and York
[210/394] (3,000). Arrears schedule of the three
Sheriffs of Yorkshire and of York city. Latin.
Variable legibility.

Subsidies
1663. Strafforth wap. and Tickhill lib. [210/390]
(750). Some decay, repaired. Some fading.
Modern contents list.
(1663). Claro wap. [210/387] (600). Some slight
decay.
1664. Staincross wap. [210/391] (200). Some
decay, repaired. Variable legibility.
Agbrigg and **Morley waps.** [262/10] (900).
1664/5. Strafforth wap. and Tickhill lib. [210/389]
(750). Considerable fading. Modern contents list.

Association Oath Rolls, 1695-6 [C.213]
[315] **Otley;** [319] **Knaresborough;** [321] **Ripon;**
[324] **New Malton;** [327] **Pontefract;**
[328] **Doncaster;** [329] **Leeds;** [331] Corporation of
Cutlers (all Yorkshire).
See also under 'Yorkshire', page 65.

West Yorkshire Archive Service, Wakefield H.Q.

Association Oath Rolls.
1698 (8 May). Eight signatories in Quarter Sessions
records [QS1/37/3, 3 of 3].

Leeds District Archives

Hearth Tax
Leeds, 1663 [Leeds Corporation Court Book,
LC/M1 p.212 foll.] (1,500). *Published.*
Bramley (Leeds) **1666**, MS copy [MD 10].

Land Tax
Sprotborough (includes Newton and part of
Cusworth), 1677, 1692, 1701, 1703 [BW/R 33].
Dacre, no date (temp. Anne) [Ingilby 3026].

Yorkshire: West Riding continued

Calderdale District Archives, Halifax

Hearth Tax
1665. Halifax and Southowram. Transcript by
John Lister of Shibden Hall; partial copy
(rearranged by number of hearths) in the *Halifax
Guardian Almanack 1903-1905* [copy in
Calderdale Reference Library].

Wakefield Metropolitan District Library

*Hearth Tax (original - the P.R.O. lists for 1672L are
based on this)*
West Riding, 1672L. Omits Pontefract. *Published.*

Sheffield Record Office

Microfilm of *Hearth Tax* returns relating to
Strafforth and Tickhill wapentake, i.e. most of
South Yorkshire. **1672L** *published.*

Doncaster Archives Department

Hearth Tax (transcript)
1672L. Lower Strafforth and Tickhill wap. [from
P.R.O. E.179/262/15] (2,500+). Indexed in main
name index. Also *published.*

Marriage Tax (originals)
Doncaster, 1706 [AB.6/1/21] (100+).

Land Tax (originals)
Doncaster Township **1700, 1703, 1710, 1712;**
Soke **1702-3** (some parishes);
Blaxton **1712** [AB.6/2/11].

Window Tax (originals)
Various townships, **1700-12** [AB.6/2/10]. These give
the amount payable, but not the number of
windows.

Barnsley Archive Service

Hearth Tax **1672L.** Microfilm of original at *Wakefield
M.D. Library.* Also *published.*

WALES

ANGLESEY

Hearth Tax (Assessments and returns)
(Transcripts at *U.C.N.W., Bangor*)

1662M. County [263/5] (?2,300). Much decay and fading. 219/26 is based on this list and is better preserved. Introduction and detailed contents list by CAFM.
1664M. County [219/26] (2,300). 1662M return for use 1664M, annotated. VG.
1670M. County [219/27] (2,750). Exempt poor shown. Beaumaris by streets. VG, but 1m. lost. Dated 2 May 1671.
1673M. County [219/28] (3,250). Exempt poor shown. Dated 8 Oct 1674.
Arrears
1662M. County [219/25] (100). Some decay.
1663M. County [219/24] (250).

Association Oath Rolls, **1695-6** [C.213]
[333] **Anglesey;** [334] **Beaumaris.**

Department of Manuscripts, The Library,
University College of North Wales, *Bangor*

Leonard Owen transcripts: *Hearth Tax*
1662M, 1664M, 1673M, County [Bangor MS.
10252, from P.R.O. E.179/263/5, 219/26,28].
1662M, 1664M, 1670M, 1673M. County [Bangor MS.13970, from P.R.O. E.179/263/5, 219/26, 219/28, 219/27].

National Library of Wales (Department of
Manuscripts), *Aberystwyth*

Marriage Tax [Carreglwyd collection]
Coedana, 1695 [369]; Llanbabo, 1695-7 [2315]; Clegyrog, parish of Llanbadrig, 1698 [848]; Llanbadrig, 1704 [760]; Llanfaes, 1701 [492]; Llanfair-yng-Nghornwy, 1700 [810]; Llanfigel, 1695-1697 [1848], 1703-4 [2241]; Llanrhwydrys, 1698-9 [1416], 1700 [912]; Llanfachreth, 1695-7 [1847], 1699 [846], 1701-2 [532], 1704 [2201]; Llanfwrog, 1703-4 [280]; Hundred of Llifon and Talybolion, 1698-9 [1463]; Hundred of Talybolian, 1704 [1417].

Aid/Land Tax
Talybolion hd., 1693-4, 1706, 1709 [Carreglwyd 98, 1191, 258, 221].

BRECONSHIRE

Free and Voluntary Present, **1661-2**
County [263/27] (3,100).

Hearth Tax (Assessments and returns)
(those available on microfilm from P.R.O. marked §)

1664L. County [263/28] (5,000). Sewn head to foot, awkward to consult. Much fading, poor legibility.
No date. County [219/63 §] (5,100). Good. Includes exempt poor.

Aid or Poll Tax
No date. County [263/29] (1,600). Some decay at feet of ms.

Association Oath Rolls, **1695-6** [C.213]
[335-37] **County;** [338] **Brecon.**

CAERNARVONSHIRE

Hearth Tax (Assessments and returns)

?1662M, 1670M. County [368/10]). Fragments, bad condition and legibility.
(Arrears)
1671. County (with Montgomery) [263/1] (150). Paper book, poor condition.

Subsidies
1663/4. County [220/161] (150). Flat. Some fading. Transcript at *U.C.N.W., Bangor*

Association Oath Rolls, **1695-6** [C.213]
[334] **County;** [345] **Caernarvon;**
[346] **Maynal Bangor.**

Caernarfon Area Record Office (Gwynedd
Archives Service), *Caernarfon*

Hearth Tax (original)
(No date, probably 1662M). County. Transcript at *U.C.N.W., Bangor.*

Department of Manuscripts, The Library,
University College of North Wales, *Bangor*

Leonard Owen transcripts:
Hearth Tax (prob. **1662M). County** [Bangor MS.13491, from *Caernarfon R.O.* original].
1664. Llanfaglan, Treflan, Llangybi, Llanarmon, Aber [9748].
c.**1664.** Clynnog, Llanllyfni, Llandwrog, Llanwno [9746].
Subsidy, **1663/4. County** [Bangor MS.13495, from P.R.O. E.179/220/161] (150).

71

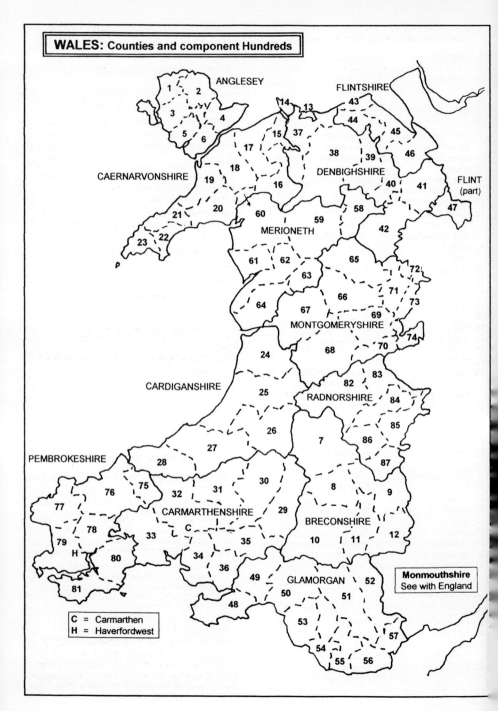

WALES: Counties and component Hundreds

ANGLESEY

FLINTSHIRE

CAERNARVONSHIRE

DENBIGHSHIRE

FLINT (part)

MERIONETH

MONTGOMERYSHIRE

CARDIGANSHIRE

RADNORSHIRE

PEMBROKESHIRE

CARMARTHENSHIRE

BRECONSHIRE

GLAMORGAN

Monmouthshire
See with England

C = Carmarthen
H = Haverfordwest

Hundreds comprising Welsh Counties

Anglesey
1. Talybolion
2. Twrcelyn
3. Llifon
4. Tyndaethwy
5. Malltraeth
6. Menai

Breconshire
7. Builth
8. Merthyr
9. Talgarth
10. Devynnock
11. Penkelly
12. Crickhowell

Caernarvonshire
13. Llysfaen and Errias
14. Creuddyn
15. Isaf
16. Nant-Conwy
17. Uchaf
18. Isgwyrfai
19. Uwchgwyrfai
20. Eifonydd
21. Dinllaen
22. Cafflogion
23. Cymdmaen

Cardiganshire
24. Genau'r Glyn
25. Ilar
26. Penarth
27. Moyddyn
28. Troedyraur

Carmarthenshire
29. Perfedd
30. Caeo/Cayo
31. Catheinog
32. Elvet
33. Derllys
34. Kidwelly
35. Iscennen
36. Carnwallon

Denbighshire
37. Isdulas
38. Isaled
39. Rhuthin/Ruthin
40. Ial/Yale
41. Maelor Bromfield
42. Chirk

Flintshire
43. Prestatyn
44. Rhuddlan
45. Coleshill
46. Mold
47. Maelor

Glamorgan
48. Swansea
49. Llangyfelach
50. Neath
51. Miskin
52. Caerphilly
53. Newcastle
54. Ogmore
55. Cowbridge
56. Dinas Powis
57. Kibbor

Merioneth
58. Edeyrnion
59. Penllyn
60. Ardudwy uwch Artro
61. Ardudwy is Artro
62. Talpont
63. Mawddwy
64. Ystumanner Estimaner

Montgomeryshire
65. Mechain Llanfyllin
66. Caereinion Mathrafel
67. Cyfeiliog Machynlleth
68. Arwystli Llanidloes
69. Cedwain Newtown
70. Ceri/Keri
71. Ystrad Marchell: Pool
72. Y.M.: Deuddwr/Deythur
73. Y.M.: Cawrse
74. Montgomery

Pembrokeshire
75. Cilgerran
76. Cemais
77. Dewsland
78. Dungleddy
79. Rhos
80. Narberth
81. Castlemartin

Radnorshire
82. Rhaeadr
83. Knighton
84. Cefnllys
85. Radnor
86. Colwyn
87. Painscastle

CARDIGANSHIRE

Public Record Office [E.179]

Free and Voluntary Present, 1661-2
County [263/43] (3,000).

Hearth Tax (Assessments and returns)
(those available on microfilm from P.R.O. marked §)

1670L. County [219/94 §] (5,000). Includes exempt poor. VG. Transcript at *Ceredigion Record Office*.
1672M. County [219/95 §] (2,500).
No date (prob. **1670's**). County [263/46 §] (5,300). Short ms. Exempt poor shown.
(Arrears)
1662M. County [219/90a] (100). Latin.
1663M. County [219/91-3] (350). Latin.
1671M-1673L. County [224/599]. 1671M for 1 yr. (140), 1673L for 1½yrs (150). Paper books.

Subsidy
(1664). County [263/44] (300).

Aid
(?1666). County [263/45] (300).

Association Oath Rolls, 1695-6 [C.213]
[339-40] **County.**

Ceredigion Record Office, Aberystwyth

Hearth Tax
1670L. Cardiganshire. Transcript of P.R.O. E.179/ 219/94 [ADX 152].

CARMARTHENSHIRE

Note: Carmarthen was assessed separately from the County.

Publications

Hearth Tax. **1670M.** County [P.R.O. E.179/220/ 128]. Extracts, *Transactions of the Carmarthenshire Antiquarian Society and Field Club:*
6 (1910-11) pp. 85-6: Extracts from 21 parishes covering all hds. except Cayo. Gives possible identification of tax payers. Exempt poor not shown (69 entries).
6, p. 92: Eglwys Cymmyn parish (21 entries; no exempt poor).
8 (1912-13), pp. 58-9, 84-6; **9** (1913-14), pp. 1-2, 39-40, 66-9: **Perfedd hd.** (1,094 entries);
10 (1914-15), pp. 66-8, 71-3: **Elvet hd.** (660).
Hearth Tax. **1671.** County [P.R.O. E.179/264/22].
Trans. C.A.S. & F.C. **7** (1911-12), pp. 1-2. Extracts from 29 parishes covering all hds. Gives possible identification of tax payers. No exempt poor. Not indexed (100 entries).

Carmarthenshire continued

Free and Voluntary Present, 1661-2
Carmarthen [264/15] (250).
Catheinog hd. [264/16] (250).
Cayo, Derllys and Kidwelly hds. [264/17]
(?1,000). Partly paper, fragile.
Elvet hd. [264/18] (500).
Perfedd hd. [264/19] (300).

Hearth Tax *(Assessments and returns)*
1670M. County [220/128] (4,850). For 1½ yrs.
Photocopy at *Carmarthenshire Record Office.*
(prob. 1670s). County [264/22] (8,000). Flattened
ms. Slight decay at feet of ms. Considerable
fading and much poor legibility. Exempt poor
shown.
(Arrears)
1663L. Carmarthen borough [375/9,10] (110).
Sperate and desperate. Latin.
1664L. County [264/21] (150). Latin. desperate.
1671M-1673M. County [224/599]. Two paper
books, 1671M, 1 yr. (375); 1673M, 1½ yrs (420).

Poll Tax (?)
(No date, W&M). County [220/130] (1,250).

Association Oath Rolls, 1695-6 [C.213]
[341] County; [342] Carmarthen; [343] Langham.

Hearth Tax
1670M. County [P'copy of P.R.O. E.179/220/128].

DENBIGHSHIRE

Publication

Hearth Tax Arrears. Desperate, **1663M** [P.R.O.
E.179/221/205] (350 collectors), *Hel Achau* (Clwyd
FHS) **13,** Summer 1984, pp.9-12, as 'Hearth Tax
Assessment for **Isaled Commote**', by W. A. Morris.

Public Record Office [E.179]

Hearth Tax *(Assessments and returns)*
1664L. County [264/36] (?10,000). Much decay,
fading; very poor legibility.
1666L. County [221/299]. Six paper books,
annotated, VG. 1, 3 and 4 are fair copies of 6.
Transcript of 1-5 at *U.C.N.W., Bangor.*
1. **(Maelor) Bromfield hd.** (3,400);
2. **Isdulas hd.** (2,000);
3. **Ruthen** and **Yale hds.** (2,500);
4. **Chirk hd.** (1,700);
5. **Denbigh hd.** (1,850);
6. **Yale, Bromfield** and **Chirk hds.** (7,600)
1671M. County (and Flintshire) [263/2] (?1,200).
Particulars of variations. Some decay, much
fading, poor legibility Isaled and Isdulas hds.
missing.

Denbighshire, P.R.O., Hearth Tax continued

No date. Bromfield hd. [264/35] (1,250). Paper
book, probably rough copy.
(Arrears)
1663M. Isaled Commote [221/205]. Desperate.
Published.

Association Oath Rolls, 1695-6 [C.213]
[347-48] County.

Leonard Owen transcripts: **Hearth Tax**
1666L. County [Bangor MS.13493, from P.R.O.
E.179/221/299].

Note. *Local Census Listings 1522-1930,* J. Gibson
and M. Medlycott, FFHS, lists two parishes in
Caernarvonshire, 32 in Denbighshire, 20 in
Flintshire and 11 in Merionethshire for which there
are population lists, mainly **1680-1** (not tax
assessments). Photocopies of these are at the
Cambridge Group for Population Studies, 27
Trumpington Street, Cambridge, CB2 1QA.

FLINTSHIRE

Hearth Tax *(Assessments and returns)*

1664M. County [221/230] (4,750). Some ms. badly
decayed, repaired, mostly OK. Annotated;
includes exempt poor. Intro. by CAFM. M/f at
Clwyd R.O. Transcript at *U.C.N.W., Bangor.*
1670M. County [264/45] (6,000). Some decay,
repaired, staining and loss of legibility, but mostly
OK. Exempt poor shown. M/f and transcript at
Clwyd R.O. Transcript also at *U.C.N.W., Bangor.*
1671M. County (and Denbighshire) [263/2].
Variations. *See under* Denbighshire.

Association Oath Rolls, 1695-6 [C.213]
[349] County; [350] Flint.

Hearth Tax
Microfilms of **1664M** [P.R.O. E.179/221/230] and
1670M [E.179/264/45].
Transcript of **1670M** [NT/61, from P.R.O.
E.179/264/45].

Leonard Owen transcripts [Bangor MS.13971]:
Hearth Tax
1664M. County [from P.R.O. E.179/221/230].
1670M. County [from P.R.O. E.179/264/45].

GLAMORGAN

Note. At the time of going to press the future of the local record offices after county re-organisation is uncertain, so prospective users should check holdings before paying visits.

Publication

The *Glamorgan* Hearth Tax assessment of *1670M*, ed. Elizabeth Parkinson. South Wales R.S., **10** (1994). Indexed.

Public Record Office [E.179]

Free and Voluntary Present, **1661-2**
County [264/470] (?5,000).

Hearth Tax (Assessments and returns)
(those available on microfilm from P.R.O. marked §; copies of asterisked records at *Glamorgan Archives Service, Cardiff.* A thesis by Elizabeth Parkinson, at the *University of Wales, College of Cardiff,* includes a transcript of *all* Glamorgan Hearth Tax returns, assessments, arrears etc.).

1670M. County [221/294 §]* (9,238). Exempt poor shown. *Published.*
1672M. Miskin hd. [221/295 §]* (600).
Parts of **Dinas Powis** and **Swansea hds.** [375/6] (1,200). Some decay, repaired.
Ogmore hd. [221/298] (114). Fragment. Flattened ms. Decay repaired. Some names illegible, others OK.
Parts of **Llangyfelach** and **Swansea hds.** [375/7] (80). Fragment.
Caerphilly hd. [221/296 §]* (600).
Neath hd. [264/48] (500).
No date (probably **1666L**). County [221/297 §]* (9,224). Flattened ms. Includes exempt poor.
(Arrears)
1664L. County [221/290 §]*(80). Latin.
1671M-1673L. County [224/599 §]*. Two paper books. 1671M, 1 year (520), 1672M-1673L, 1½ years (500).

Aid
No date. County [276/47B] (650).

Association Oath Roll, **1695-6** [C.213]
[351] County.

Glamorgan Archives Service, Cardiff

Hearth Tax
Microfilm of **County 1666L** (prob.) [P.R.O. E.179/ 221/297]; **1670M** [221/294], **1672M** [221/295-6]; arrears: **1664L** [221/290], **1671M-1673L** [224/599]. Microfilm also available at *University of Wales, College of Cardiff.*
Transcripts: **1666L?** Ystradyfodwg; **1666L?** and **1670M**. Aberdare.

Glamorgan continued

University of Wales, Cardiff

Hearth Tax
A transcript of *all* Glamorgan Hearth Tax returns, assessments, arrears etc. forms part of thesis by Elizabeth Parkinson.

West Glamorgan Archive Service, Swansea

Hearth Tax
1670M County [Microfilm of P.R.O. E.179/221/294].
1672? County.
Arrears: **1671M County** [Microfilm of 224/599].

MERIONETH

Publication

'The *Hearth Tax* of **1662M** in **Merioneth'**, [P.R.O. E.179/265/2] (1,950), by Owen Parry, *Jnl. of the Merioneth Historical and Record Soc. (Clychgrawn Cwmdeithas Hanes a Chofnodion Sir Feironnydd),* vol. 2, pt. 1, 1953-6, pp.16-38. Lists compiled by petty and high constables. Missing: Ystumaner, Llanbedr, Llanfihangel, Llanfrothen and Llanaber in Ardydwy. Not indexed.

Public Record Office [E.179]

Hearth Tax (Assessments and returns)

1662M. County [265/2] (1,950). *Published.* Some decay, repaired, considerable staining and some poor legibility, but mostly OK.
1666L. County [222/400a] (4,500). Paper book, annotated. Parry comments: 'names anglicized, work of a stranger'. Transcript at *U.C.N.W., Bangor.*
(Arrears)
1663M. County [375/39] (100).

Subsidy
(1663). County [222/331] (300). Sewn head to foot Transcript at *U.C.N.W., Bangor.*

Aid
(1664-6). County [222/332] (?500-1,000). Transcript at *U.C.N.W., Bangor.*

Association Oath Roll, **1695** [C.213]
[352] County.

Department of Manuscripts, The Library, University College of North Wales, Bangor

Leonard Owen transcripts [Bangor MS.13494]:
Hearth Tax
1666L. County [from P.R.O. E.179/222/400a].
Subsidy
(1663). County [from P.R.O. E.179/222/331].
Aid
(1664-6). County [from P.R.O. E.179/222/332].

Monmouthshire - see with England, page 43.

MONTGOMERYSHIRE

Public Record Office [E.179]

Hearth Tax *(Assessments and returns)*
(Transcripts at *U.C.N.W., Bangor*)

1662M. County [265/7] (6,000). Some decay, repaired, considerable fading and staining, some poor legibility, but mostly OK. Introduction and detailed contents list by CAFM.
1671. County [265/10] (6,200). Exempt poor shown. Transcript at *Society of Genealogists*.
(Arrears)
1663M. County [265/9] (50). Latin.
1671. County (with Caernarvonshire) [263/1] (250). Paper book.

Subsidies
(Transcripts at *U.C.N.W., Bangor*)
1663. County [265/8] (300). Flat. Considerable decay, not repaired; some fading.
(1667). Deythur, Llanfyllin, Machynlleth, Mathrafel and Pool hds. [223/403] (200). Bad decay, repaired. Many names lost.

Poll Tax
(1665-6). County [223/405] (1,700). Transcript at *U.C.N.W., Bangor*.
(1697). County [223/406] (150). Collectors' names only.

Association Oath Rolls, 1695-6 [C.213]
[353] **County**; [354] **Montgomery**;
[355] **Welshpool**.

Department of Manuscripts, The Library, University College of North Wales, Bangor

Leonard Owen transcripts [Bangor MS.13974]:

Hearth Tax
1662M. County [from P.R.O. E.179/265/7].
1671. County [from P.R.O. E.179/265/10].

Subsidies
1663. County [from P.R.O. E.179/265/8].
(1667). Deythur, Llanfyllin, Machynlleth, Mathrafel and **Pool hds.** [from P.R.O. E.179/223/403].

Poll Tax
(1665-6). County [from P.R.O. E.179/223/405].

Society of Genealogists, London

Hearth Tax: 1671. County [from P.R.O. E.179/265/10]. TS transcript. Not indexed. Wrongly described as 1680.

PEMBROKESHIRE

Note: Haverfordwest was assessed separately from the County.

Publications

Hearth Tax, **1670M, County** [P.R.O. E.179/ 224/532 except for m.44], in 'Pembrokeshire Hearths in 1670', *West Wales Historical Records.* Exempt poor shown. Excludes Haverfordwest. Indexed by Dyfed FHS.
Vol. **9** (1920-23), pp. 217-40: Kilgarron hd.; Roose hd. (part) (1,700).
Vol. **10** (1924), pp. 177-216: Roose hd., continued: Castlemartin, Dongleddy hds.; Dewsland hd. (part) (3,000).
Vol. **11** (1926), pp. 113-40: Dewsland hd., contd.: Narberth hd. (1,600).

Public Record Office [E.179]

Free and Voluntary Present, 1661-2
County [265/18] (2,400). Ms. head to foot.

Hearth Tax *(Assessments and returns)*
(those available on microfilm from P.R.O. marked §)

1670M. County [224/532] (6,300). *Published.*
1671M. County [375/41] (?6,500). In six parts. Much decay, repaired, and fading. Leg. variable.
(Arrears)
1671M-1673L. County [224/599 §]. Two paper books. 1671M (500); 1673L (500).

Subsidy or Aid (?)
(1666). County [224/530] (680). Flat.

Association Oath Rolls, 1695-6 [C.213]
[356-57] **County**; [358] **Pembroke**;
[359] **Haverfordwest**; [360] **Tenby**.

Pembrokeshire Record Office, Haverfordwest.

Haverfordwest: *Poll Tax,* **1698;**
Window Tax, **1707** (St. Mary's only);
Land Tax, **1698-1721.**

RADNORSHIRE

Public Record Office [E.179]

Free and Voluntary Present, 1661-2
County [265/22] (2,500).

Hearth Tax *(Assessments and returns)*

No date. County [224/593] (3,600). Short ms. Includes exempt poor.
[265/23] (150). Fragments, for Llanbister, Llanbadarn, Broylis only. Exempt poor shown. Some fading, some decay, not repaired.

Aid
(1666). County [224/591] (250).

Association Oath Rolls, 1695-6 [C.213]
[361-63] **County;** [364] **Radnor.**

SCOTLAND

Although Scotland was of course not subject to taxes levied by the English parliament, there were similar taxes during the later Stuart period. Chief amongst these were the **Hearth Tax** of **1691** and the **Poll Tax** Rolls, **1694-1699**. These have been briefly described in *Sources for Scottish Genealogy and Family History*, D.J. Steel (*National Index of Parish Registers*, vol. **12**), 1970, pp. 121-24, 171-74 (based on articles by J.F. Mitchell and William Rodger first published in the *Scottish Genealogist*, **10**, 4 and **11**, 3, 1964). However since then the Scottish Record Society has published an authoritative volume relating to the Hearth Tax, on which much of the information given here is, by kind permission, based.

Hearth Tax

This tax is fully descibed and discussed in *West Lothian Hearth Tax 1691; with county abstracts for Scotland*, ed. Duncan Adamson, Scottish Record Society, N.S. **9**, 1981. Although its collection in some cases took several years, the tax was levied in relation to 1691, and the names listed are those who were the householders on Candlemas day, 1691. In some cases, however, usually towns, the lists instead refer to the autumn of 1690. The records are all now in the **Scottish Record Office**, *H.M. General Register House, Edinburgh EH1 1EW.*

The only returns published are those for Dumfriesshire, southern Perthshire and Stirling-shire, and West Lothian.

The second part of the S.R.S. volume describes, county by county, the returns for each, giving the name of the subcollector; the 'Nature of the Record': a detailed description of the content of the returns and geographical arrangement; the S.R.O. reference; date it was deponed; a list of all parishes/places, in the order in which they appear, and their number of hearths; and the total number of hearths. In the county entries that follow, the S.R.O. references are shown in square brackets and the number of hearths (*not* householders) in round brackets, both taken from the S.R.S. volume.

Poll Tax, 1694-1699

The most accessible description of this important record is probably that by D.J. Steel in *Sources for Scottish Genealogy and Family History*, pp. 121-24. Amount of detail varies, but at best, all the household may be named. The records (originals or mifrofilm) for which references are given are in the *Scottish Record Office* unless shown otherwise. Published tran-scripts are given under county entries.

HT = Hearth Tax; **PT** = Poll Tax

Aberdeenshire: HT [E69/1-12] (27,102 - but totals only, no names).
PT: *List of Pollable Persons within the Shire of Aberdeen, 1696,* pub. 1844, 2 vols. All parishes [Aberdeen Univ. Archives MS.548]. New edition by Aberdeen and NE Scotland FHS: Lonmay, Old Deer and Long Side, Aberdeen and Freedom Lands, Peterculter, Strathbogie (2 vols.) pubd. Remainder in preparation.
1694. Kearn [GD.52/6].
1698. Alford, Tough, Leochel, Cushnie, Tullynessle, Forbes, Kearn, Clatt and Kennethmont [GD.52/7].
1699. Same parishes [GD.52/8].

Angus - *see* Forfarshire.

Argyll and Bute: HT [E69/3; GD1112/10/10 (Breadalbane papers)] (6,539 - names given, except for Mull, Tiree, Coll, Ardnamurchan, Sunart, Appin, Glencoe, Canna and Morvern, 'being in rebellion').
PT [records from the Argyll Sheriff Court, now in West Register House]:
1698. Islay [SC/54/19/44/3].
1699. Kilfinnan, Kintyre, Kilmichael-Glassary and Kilmartin [SC/54/19/44/4,6,7]. Very few names in either.

Ayrshire: HT. Carrick [E69/2/2] (2,339 - taxpayers' names only); Kyle [E69/2/1] (5,836) - variable record of taxpayers' names); Cunningham [E69/2/3/] (5,750) - taxpayers' names).
PT. 1698. Largs [E70/1(2)].
1699. Barr, Dailly, Girvan [E70/1(1)]. Very few names in either.

Banffshire: HT [E69/4/1-2] (3,249 - but totals only. no names).
PT: List of persons deficient in payment of PT of 1695, dated 1697 [Banffshire Sheriff Court Records]. Printed in *Transactions of Banffshire Field Club*, **24** (1903-4), pp. 3-18.

Berwickshire: HT [E69/5; GD26/7/359] (5,470) - taxpayers' names only).
PT. 1695. Ayton, Edrom, Eyemouth, Greenlaw, Polwarth [Fraser Charters DG/86/770A]. All give occupations and location of houses. Greenlaw also lists wives and children. Mitchell/Steel also lists Swinton, not on S.R.O. list.
Hutton [Hume of Marchmont collection, GD.158/679]. Names wives, children, occupations, location of houses.
Lauder [E70/2/1]. Very few names.

Bute - *see* Argyll.

Caithness: HT [GD26/7/373] (3,348 - but totals only, no names).

SCOTLAND, continued

Clackmannanshire: HT [E69/6] (1,442 - of which 190 are un-named poor).

Dumfriesshire: HT [GD26/7] (about 7,500). Tax lists and analysis (ed. Duncan Adamson) published in *Transactions of the Dumfries and Galloway Natural History Society*, vols. 47-9 (1970-2).

Dunbartonshire: HT [E69/7] (2,882 - names of householders, farm by farm, but total only for Dumbarton (282)).

East Lothian: HT. Haddington Presbytery [E69/9/2-4] (8,733) - taxpayers named, but not 611 poor); Dunbar Presbytery [E69/9/1/] (1,947 - taxpayers named).
PT. 1698. Dirleton [E70/3]. Few names.

Edinburgh and Leith: HT [E69/16/2-3] (19,624 - individual names given).
PT. 1694. [E70/4/1-11]. Canongate (wives, occupations); College Kirk (wives); Greyfriars (wives, imperfect); Lady Yester's (wives, imperfect); New Kirk (children, imperfect); Old Kirk (children); West Kirk (St. Cuthbert's (occupations, location of houses); North Leith (occupations); South Leith (imperfect); Tolbooth (wives, children, occupations); Tron Kirk (wives, children, occupations).
[Edinburgh Town Council records]:
1694. 1. Tolbooth; 2. Old Kirk. Published in *Edinburgh Poll Tax Returns for 1694*, ed. Marguerite Wood, Scottish Record Soc., 1951. Indexed. See also 'Edinburgh Poll Tax Returns' by Marguerite Wood, in *Book of the Old Edinburgh Club*, **25**, pp. 90-120.
1695. 3-5. Old Kirk; Greyfriars; New Kirk;
1698. 6. Lady Yester's parish; 7. College Kirk; 8. New Kirk.
1699. 9. New Kirk.
See also Midlothian.

Elgin - see Moray.

Fife and Kinross: HT. Dunfermline Presbytery [E69/10/1] (4,485 - of which 282 are un-named poor); Presyteries of St. Andrews, Cupar and Kircaldy [E69/10/2] (15,376 paid and named; 739 poor or deficient, un-named).
PT. 1695-6. Anstruther Wester [original in Anstruther Town Council records, transcript at S.R.O., RH.2/1/68]. Names wives, children, occupations.
1698. Aberdour, Wemyss [E70/5/1,2]. Very few names.
No date. St. Andrews [original in St. Andrews burgh records, B/65/20/2]; ? transcript at S.R.O.

Forfarshire (Angus) (including parts of modern Perthshire): HT [E69/11/1] (14,000 but often block estate totals rather than individual names).

Haddington - see East Lothian.

Inverness-shire: HT [E69/12/1] (6,789 - generally in block totals, headed by heritors' names; names of 151 individual poor are given).
PT. 1699. Inverness burgh (118 names, occupation, location of houses); other places named: Brarban, Croy, Daviol, Moy, Dunlechity, Dallarsie, Durvis, Ballieskin, Abertariff, Urquhart and Glenmoriston, Ward Law, Kiltarlie, Killincrack (?), Strathspey, Rothiemurchis, Kingussie, Allowe, Culloden, Kilfinnan, Isle of Skye [E70/6/1] (156 names, excl. Inverness).

Kincardineshire: HT [E69/13] (4,033 - of which 405 are un-named poor).

Kinross - see Fife.

Stewartry of Kirkcudbright: HT [E69/14] (3,364 - but block totals grouped by estate only, no names).

Lanarkshire (Clydesdale): HT [E69/15] (19,196 - but variable for detail; some parishes give all names, some just those that paid. In the south, the record is very poor, usually in blocks under heritors; some parishes, including Glasgow, give only total).
PT.1695. Lesmahagow, published in *Annals of the Parish of Lesmahagow*, by J.B. Greenshields, 1864, pp. 163-85 [original in private collection; lists for the remainder of the Upper Ward of Lanarkshire existed mid-C19, but present location probably unknown].
Burgh of Glasgow, deficients only [E70/7/4].
1698. Barony (Glasgow), Bothwell, Cadder, Cambuslang, Carmunnock, Govan, Lanark, Lemahagow, Rutherglen [E70/7/1-3]. Very few names.
1699-1700? Burgh of Glasgow (incomplete) [E70/7/5].

Linlithgowshire - see West Lothian.

Midlothian: HT [E69/16/1] (10,920 - but variable for detail. Individuals named in some parishes, block estate totals only for others).
PT. [E70/8]. (a = wives named; b = children named; c = occupations given; d = locations of houses given).
1694. Carrington (a,b,c); Cockpen (a,b,c), pubd. in *Scottish Genealogist*, **19**, 2 (June 1972), pp. 63-8; Cramond (a,b,d); Cranston and Falla (c); Dalkeith and Lasswade (d), Lasswade pubd. in *Scot. Gen.*, **28**, 3 (Sept 81), pp. 122-39; Duddingston (d); Inveresk (c); Kirknewton (c,d); Liberton (b,c,d); Newbattle (imperfect; a,b,c); Penicuik (b,c,d); Ratho (a,b,c,d); Stow (a,b,c,d); Temple (c).
No date. Borthwick (b,c,d); Colinton (imperfect; a,c); Crichton (b,c,d); Currie (imperfect; a,c); Calderclare or East Calder (d); Heriot (b,c); Mid Calder (b,c); West Calder (c,d).
See also Edinburgh, Leith and Canongate.

SCOTLAND, continued

Moray (Elgin) **and Nairn: HT** [E69/17] (2,545 - but block totals only, no names).
PT. 1698 [E70/9(1) 'List for shire']. Ardclach (7), Auldearn (14), Calder (6), Croy (3), Nairn (3).

Orkney and Shetland. HT. Shetland only [GD26/7/327] (1,786 - but totals only, no names). None for Orkney.
PT. 1695-6. Orkney only [Orkney and Shetland collection (Register House), 2 vols. RH.9/15/175]. All parishes (wives, children, occupations, houses, for some parishes only).
1698. [E.70/10(1)]. Kirkwall burgh.

Peebles - see with Selkirkshire.

Perthshire. HT. Perth and Dunkeld Presbyteries [E69/1-4] (15,371); Dunblane and Auchterarder Presbyteries with Culross and Tulliallan parishes: [? ref.] (9,027). Southern Perthshire hearth books are included with the gravestone survey published by the Scottish Genealogy Society.
PT. 1694. [B59/22/24]. Perth burgh.
1695. [Rollo of Duncrub MSS, GD.56/128, Register House]. Part of Dunning (Dalreoch and Ballgouer pertaining to the Laird of Gleneagles).
[Fergusson of Baledmund muniments.] Persons belonging to John Fergusson of Dunfallandie.
1696. [GD.316/10] Parish of Errol.

Renfrewshire. HT. [E69/20] (5,473 - individuals named in Houston).
PT. 1695. All parishes in county [?formerly in Paisley Town Council records]. Publ. in *Glasgow Herald*, 1864. Copies of set of cuttings at Paisley Library (indexed); S.R.O. [T.335, Printed Books catalogue]; Glasgow University Library; Scottish Society of Antiquaries; and British Library.
Kilmacolm and **Kilbarchan** pub. by the New Society, vols. **10** and **12. Paisley** in *A History of Paisley, 1660-1908*, by W.M. Metcalfe, 1909; **Kilbarchan** in *Kilbarchan: A Parish History*, R.D. Mackenzie, 1902; **Kilmacolm**, in *Kilmacolm*, J. Murray, 1907; **Neilston** in *History of the Parish of Neilston*, D. Pride, 1910.
1694-6. [E70/12]. Houston (children, occupations); Inchinnan (imperfect; wives, children); Kilbarchan (wives, children, houses); Killellan (occupations, houses); Kilmacolm (wives, children, occupations).
These lists sometimes have material additional to that published.

Ross and Cromarty: HT [GD26/7/391] (3,695 - totals only, no names).
Roxburghshire: HT [E69/21] (7,101 - of which 391 are un-named poor).

Selkirkshire and Peebleshire (Forest and Tweeddale): **HT** [E69/18] (3,447 - but generally block totals under estates, no names).
PT. 1694 [SC.42/5/1. Peebles: Lintoun, Skurling, Barns, Cringellie, Blackbanonie, Countess of Mortoun, Haystoun.
Selkirks: [Horsburgh paper GD.178/box 2]. Selkirk, 1694, 1695 (?also Ettrick).

Shetland - see with Orkney.

Stirlingshire: HT [E69/22/1] (8,114 - varies from a very detailed record for Stirling burgh to parishes which do not give individual names at all). Stirlingshire hearth books are included with the gravestone survey *published* by the Scottish Genealogy Society.

Sutherland. HT [E69/23] (2,313 - individuals named in most parishes).

West Lothian [Linlithgowshire]. **HT** [E69/24/1-2] (5.968) *Published*, Scottish Record Society, N.S., vol. **9**, 1981, pp. 7-70. Indexed.
PT. 1694 [E70/13] (a = wives named; b = children named; c = occupations given; d = locations of houses given).
Abercorn (imperfect; a,b); Bathgate (c,d); Bo'ness and Kinneill (a,b,c); Carriden (imperfect; a,b,c,d); Dalmeny (b,c,d); Ecclesmachen (imperfect; a,b); Kirkliston (a,b,c,d); Livingston (b,c,d); Torpichen (c,d); Uphall or Strathbrook (imperfect; a,b).

Wigtownshire. HT [E69/25] (3,458 - arranged by proprietors, not parishes; almost all paying the tax are named. The poor are listed separately).
PT. 1699. [E70/14(1)]. List of polled persons omitted (12).

IRELAND

Information on *Hearth Taxes* in Ireland is based on that given by Rosemary ffolliott in her paper 'Irish Census Returns and Census Substitutes', published in *Irish Genealogy: A Record Finder*, ed. Donal F. Begley, Heraldic Artists, Dublin.

Hearth Tax

Co. Antrim. 1669 [Nat.Lib.Ms.9584 and P.R.O.N.I.].
Co. Armargh. 1664 [GO.538,Nat Lib.Ms.9586 and P.R.O.N.I.]. Also printed in *Archivum Hibernicum*, vol. **8**, 1936.
Co. Cavan. 1664 for parishes of Killeshandra, Kildallan, Killenagh, Templeport, Tomregan [P.R.O.N.I.].
Co. Donegal. 1665 [GO.538 and Nat.Lib. Ms.9584 and P.R.O.N.I.].
Co. Dublin. 1663. Printed in *Jnl. of Kildare Arch. Soc.*, vol. **10**. See also 'A List of Residents in the County of Dublin in 1664', extracted from Hearth Tax rolls by Capt. G.S. Cory. TS at *Society of Genealogists*.
Co. Fermanagh. 1665 [Nat.Lib.Ms.9583].
Co. Kilkenny. 1664. 37 parishes (listed in *Irish Genealogy*, as above). [Transcript in the Carrigan Mss., Kilkenny.] Printed in the *Irish Genealogist*, vol. **5**, nos.1 and 2, 1974-5.
Co. Londonderry. 1663 [Nat.Lib.Ms.9584].
Co. Louth. 1663-4. Printed in the *Jnl. of the Co. Louth Arch.Soc.*, vol. **6**, nos. 2 and 4.
1666-7. Dunleer parish. Printed in *The Irish Genealogist*, 1969.
Co. Monaghan. 1666. Printed in *A History of Monaghan*, by D.C. Rushe.
Co. Sligo. 1664. Printed in *Analecta Hibernica*, **24**, 1967 (Irish MSS.Comm.)
Co. Tipperary. 1666, 1667, 1668. Three rolls. Printed as *Tipperary's Families*, ed. Thomas Laffan, Dublin, 1911.
Co. Tyrone. 1664 [Nat.Lib.Ms 9583-4]. (The portion covering Clogher diocese was printed in *The Clogher Record*, 1965).
(**Co. Waterford. 1663.** Inhabitants of Waterford city, showing trade or profession, printed in the *Jnl. of Cork Hist. and Arch. Soc.*, vol. **51**).
Co. Westmeath. 1666. Mullingar only. Printed in the *Franciscan College Journal*, 1950.
Co. Wicklow. 1669. [G.O.667].

No records survive for the counties of Carlow, Clare, Cork, Down, Galway, Kerry, Kildare, King's County (Offaly), Leitrim, Limerick, Longford, Mayo, Meath, Queen's County (Leix), Roscommon and Wexford.

ASSOCIATION OATH ROLLS, 1695-6

Categories of oath-takers not included under English or Welsh counties.

Publications

The Association Oath Rolls of the British Plantations (New York, Virginia, etc.) A.D. 1696, ed. Wallace Gandy, 1922. Indexed. Includes all 'Foreign Plantations' [P.R.O. C.213/459-61, 465-72. but not 462-64 (Jersey, Guernsey, Scilly Isles)].
Did Your Ancestors Sign the Jersey Oath of Association Roll of 1696?: A History of the Roll and Many of the People Who Signed It, Alex Glendinning, The Channel Islands FHS, 1995. From P.R.O. C.213/462 (2,975). Transcript of all names. plus facsimiles of documents and signatures, and biographical details of very many of those named. Partial index (to those named in text, *not* to all in the transcribed lists). A very ambitious and informative book.

Public Record Office [C.213]

[1] House of Commons;
[365-402] Various officers, civil and military, including the whole Civil Service, Yeomen of the Guard, some military and naval men and the 'Nobility and Gentry'.
[403-458] Clergy, arranged under diocese and deanery.

Foreign Plantations etc.
[459] King's subjects in **Holland**;
[460] English Factory at **Malaga**;
[461] English merchants in **Geneva**;
[462] **Jersey**; [463] **Guernsey**;
[464] **Scilly Isles** - see Cornwall, page 19;
[465] **Barbados**, Governor and Council;
[466] Clergy; [467] Officers of the Regiment;
[468] **Virginia**, St. James City Burgesses;
[469] **New York Province**, Governor and Council;
[470] **New York City**, Mayor, Recorder and Commonalty.
[471] **Bermuda Islands**;
[472] **Leeward Islands**.